7 Secrets
of Confidence

Also by Steve Miller

Get Off Your Arse & Lose Weight
Change Your Life – Grab That Job

7 Secrets
of Confidence

Straight-talking advice on how
to become more confident

STEVE MILLER

<u>headline</u>

First published in 2010 by
HEADLINE PUBLISHING GROUP

1

Cataloguing in Publication Data is available from the British Library

ISBN 978 07553 1953 4

Typeset in Bell MT by Avon DataSet Ltd,
Bidford-on-Avon, Warwickshire

Printed in Great Britain by CPI Mackays, Chatham, ME5 8TD

Headline's policy is to use papers that are natural, renewable and
recyclable products and made from wood grown in sustainable forests.
The logging and manufacturing processes are expected to conform
to the environmental regulations of the country of origin.

HEADLINE PUBLISHING GROUP
An Hachette UK Company
338 Euston Road
London NW1 3BH

www.headline.co.uk
www.hachette.co.uk

My books are dedicated to the life and wise words of
my very special friend June Linda Thompson.
Your guidance and support continues to inspire me
and our exciting journey continues . . .

Create, believe, expect and it can happen.

Acknowledgements

To the experts:
Eddie Bell, my agent
Jason Stratford-Lysandrides, my lawyer
Emily Furniss, my publicist
Wendy McCance, my publisher
Matt Rowlands, for creative spark
Yu-kuang Chou, a top photographer
David Rabone, my friend and professional buddy
Lindsey Gibson, a fabulous stylist
Jackie Lowe and Janet Smith, my friends and business guides

To the friends:
You know who you are and I love you all

To the family:
Alan Possart, for standing by me throughout
Terry Brookes, a rock
Mum, Dad, Julie, Paul and my awesome niece and nephew
Amy and Ryan

CONTENTS

Off You Go!

Preface

This book was written because I feel that many people around the world need to restore their confidence, which has been knocked down by the slings and arrows that we all have to face. There are so many big problems that are out of our control these days, from economic bubbles bursting to natural disasters brought on by climate change. Never before have there been so many daily tests of confidence for people.

I want to offer people who need to build or rebuild their confidence a tool that is practical, action-based and immediate. For too long we have simply listened to the theory from head-in-the-clouds, head-up-their-backside therapists and life coaches. I'm all about delivering a product that offers real-world, here-and-now solutions to building and maintaining confidence.

For years I struggled with my own confidence, which eventually led me to suffer from pretty awful panic attacks. I knew I had to take quick action to correct this debilitating life state; I had to do something which had a real impact on my outlook and my confidence. But sitting on a therapist's couch analysing the past or booking time with a wishy-washy life coach wasn't the answer. In fact, I know now that in my case it would have made the situation worse!

To get myself out of the rut I'd got trapped in, I came up with several simple approaches to boosting my confidence and getting off my backside to take my life forward. The approaches I used became my 7 Secrets of Confidence. Well, they aren't secrets now, as I'm going to share them with you in this logical journey to building and expanding personal confidence.

When I decided to put the book together, I also decided to commission YouGov, the internationally respected survey and pollster organisation, to help identify the UK's top ten priorities when it comes to improving self-confidence. This was interesting and opened my eyes to the major issues that people face which challenge the confidence they have. By identifying these priorities, I could see that the 7 Secrets which helped me to master my self-confidence are the basis for practical strategies to help anyone increase long-term confidence.

Having trained professionally in clinical hypnosis, I also offer in this book a series of hypnotic scripts designed to help increase confidence in the top ten areas. The scripts may be read to you by someone else or you may choose to read them to yourself daily. What you read will be a number of carefully constructed positive suggestions to help build your confidence in many areas of your personal and professional life. Please note, however, that readers suffering from clinical depression or epilepsy should consult their GPs before using the scripts.

For the last ten years, I have worked with a wide range of people seeking effective and easy-to-use techniques to kick-start their confidence. This client work has encouraged me to develop a three-session process that has successfully delivered results for hundreds of people, including business executives, celebrities, actors, sports professionals, entrepreneurs and members of the public. In this book I share some of my experiences with them, offering you an insight into the confidence issues of people from all walks of life and the techniques I use and advice I give to help them feel supremely confident.

If you've read any of my other books dealing with weight loss and finding your ideal job, or read about me, you will know that my way of doing things is to cut through the rubbish that a lot of 'experts' bandy around. The advice and tips you will pick up are direct and designed to get you to take action and take command of your confidence. This is very serious stuff, but you will also find that I like to have a light-hearted look at the world and myself from time to time, so I know you will have fun and come away as the 'captain of your confidence'.

I want you to enjoy this book, but most of all I want you to move forward and bolster your confidence in both your personal and professional life.

For a personal consultation email me at info@stevemiller training.com. Further details can be found at www.stevemiller training.com.

Introduction: How I Unlocked the 7 Secrets

Years ago I set out to research and define exactly what confidence is all about. However, I soon realised it's a tricky trait to pin down. I attempted to come up with my own definitions and labels, but gave up after writing about 20 of them. I couldn't quite put my finger on what confidence is. Run your mouse across the internet and you will find a range of mind-boggling definitions that will only serve to confuse the issue.

Definitions range from 'freedom from doubt' to 'belief in yourself and your abilities', with dozens in between. But with surveys revealing that up to 75 per cent of people are crying out for an increase in their self-confidence, whatever confidence may be, most of us need to learn to command it. The word 'confidence' actually comes from the Latin for 'to put one's trust in someone', in this case that someone being ourselves. Putting trust in ourselves is now the way I like to see confidence. We command our confidence to act for us when we use a number of tools which may appear to be a mystery to many, but which I will take you through, so that you can 'trust yourself' and be confident.

" Up to 75 per cent of people are crying out for an increase in their self-confidence **"**

Are you a confident person? Have a look at this simple confidence checklist.

	Always	Sometimes	Never
When you meet someone for the first time, do you make immediate eye contact?			
Do you hold your head up and walk tall in public?			
Do you offer a firm handshake to strangers?			
Is your face relaxed when meeting new people?			
When you talk in public and to new people is your voice clear?			
Is your breathing relaxed and even in unfamiliar surroundings?			
Are you a decisive decision-maker?			

The one thing that is certain is that without confidence life is a real battle. It has to be, because confidence influences everything we do, from how we talk to those around us to looking people in the eye. Without confidence, approaching anything in life is a challenge. Without the right level of confidence, you are doomed to be a loser. Confidence makes us feel good about ourselves; it helps shape positive behaviours, and supports us to be the best we can in everything that we do. So without spouting lots of theories, how do we command it? Is it something that just happens by luck or does it have a trigger?

The answer is simple. Confidence is something you can both think and feel. And it doesn't take a genius to work out that what you think is what you feel. It is our thoughts that determine what we feel, otherwise known as emotions, and it is our emotions that determine our behaviour. So, quite simply put, the way you think will determine how confident you feel. So what triggers thought? That's also a simple one – you do. We think constantly when we are awake and the person choosing the thoughts is you. We think about so many things. It could be about the way you look, the way you sound, your desire to try new things, your ambitions and even the partner you deserve.

> **Confidence is something you feel**

It's vital to remember that it's you and no one else who determines your thoughts. No doubt you will all have heard the tried and tested cliché: 'Is your glass half full or half empty?' But this is true. So we come to the point that confidence is totally underpinned by your own thought processes and nobody else's. And if you are one of those people who blame others for the way you feel, then cut it out right now, because you've got to get your thinking sorted! It may be a hard one to swallow, but swallow it you must. This is the ground rule we'll follow – it's you who is firing off the thought processes in your mind, you pull the trigger and can start to control the aim, and right now we're aiming straight at self-confidence.

To start to get on target in supporting your own thoughts, there are actions you can take so that what you think about yourself acts to command your confidence. I emphasise 'action' because lazy, can't-be-bothered types will always remain victims in life. Why? Because they take no responsibility for themselves. They expect others to do it for them and often lash out at others for making them they way they are. Listen out for them. They do nothing practical to help themselves and will sit on their arses moaning and whinging about the way their life is and how others make them feel. Keep clear of these drains or 'suckers', as they will poison your own personal growth, latch on to your energy and, quite frankly, you will end up feeling down and empty. These people don't want to command their confidence; they just want to wallow deep in self-pity, doing their best to wreck not only themselves but also those around them.

With that point made, you will now move forward, taking action to help turn any negative thoughts that you have about yourself into positives, so that you command your confidence to act in your interests. Throughout the book, you will go through my 7 Secrets of Confidence. I will guide you through a number of exercises that will help you to take control of your confidence so that those around you admire you and aspire to your behaviours and actions. So let's get excited, get into the learning zone and be prepared for action.

As you will have gathered, this is a take-action book and so, in my normal fashion, you won't be sitting on your fat backside doing nothing; you will be up on your feet a lot of the time, doing stuff that will make a difference rather than just mulling things over in your head. So right now you should be getting really excited about the prospect of commanding your confidence. And if you aren't shouting, 'Yes! Yes! Yes!' similar to when you are in the throes of passion, then try harder. As I underlined earlier, in no uncertain terms, this is down to you.

The Magnificent 7

Fifteen years ago, while driving south on the M6 from Manchester to Birmingham, I can recall feeling a sudden intensity of fear and a dizziness that I can only describe as an omen of impending death. Quickly pulling over on the hard shoulder, I dialled for help. I was soon to discover this was the start of what would be the worst 12 months of my life. My GP informed me that I was suffering from panic attacks and, in their tired fashion, prescribed medication.

Playing the victim and taking months off work is not my style and I knew medication alone was not the answer. I soon realised that my confidence had been destroyed and torn up into little pieces. While I had close friends and a supportive family, I felt so alone. This can be the worst feeling: that you are alone and isolated and that no one will come and help you. The panic symptoms became a daily recurrence and I became more desperate to find a resolution to this debilitating state. Hiding away was not the answer and, as hard as it was, I decided to take action. I decided to quit my job, return to Birmingham and start life afresh. It was one of the biggest risks in life I had taken, but I just knew it was the right thing to do.

> Playing the victim and taking
> months off work is not my style

It was from here that I developed my 7 Secrets of Confidence. I had gotten fed up of popping anti-depressants that just spaced me out and acted like a bandage over a festering wound. Enough was enough – I knew the infection had set in and I didn't want to develop blood poisoning, so I decided to sit down and develop an action plan that covered seven crucial points. All of the seven have now become an integral part of the way I live my life. I want you to open the door and let them into your life, experience the benefits and let them become the pillars that maintain your self-confidence as high as it can go.

These secrets are described in the chapters that follow. I will offer you a number of techniques, tips and actions for each of the secrets, so there's no room for crappy excuses for not commanding your confidence.

Here is a quick summary of the secrets, so you can start to get them into your mind and your life:

1   The past is past – letting go of what has gone before and building on what will be a terrific and fulfilling future.

2   Wave goodbye to perfection – realising that it is okay not to be perfect and noticing how much better you become.

3   Chill – conditioning yourself to be relaxed about yourself and the world around you.

4   Sort your head out – building self-belief in your brilliance.

5   Brand yourself brilliant – you are a visible product.

6   Stretch – stepping out of the comfort zone to prove you can do it.

7   Copycat – modelling yourself on the best.

These are my 'Magnificent 7' and they will act as the tools you use to build and protect your confidence from now on. Every time you feel like bowing your head, avoiding people and so on, just remember you have got the Magnificent 7 to draw on and feel really confident.

Real Life

James

James, 36, was a senior manager working in publishing. Four months before visiting me he had been promoted to a new position managing a large team. He was a handsome guy and I could see potential charisma. However, for James the pressure was on, with advertisement revenues diving month after month as the economic downturn hit home. As his own sales record took a tumble, James felt that his personal confidence was diminishing fast and he knew something had to be done. Full of anxiety, James decided to contact me to engage me as his personal confidence coach.

He explained to me that he was becoming flaky in management team meetings and not able to communicate in the motivational manner to which he had become accustomed. As someone who had always had the wow factor, he couldn't afford to lose it, especially at a time when commercial results were so critical.

The goals were clearly set to make James become what he had always previously been: a dynamic leader who inspired those around him to achieve results. His self-belief had collapsed lower than most stocks in the FTSE 100, his image was dull, and he twitched all the way through our first meeting like a card-carrying anorak seeing his first eagle through his binos. In short, James was thinking like crap, so he therefore performed like crap. Applying all the 7 Secrets to help James command his confidence, it took just two short months for him to report a surge in self-esteem, a more focused leadership style, communication skills that again inspired and an upturn in advertisement revenues against his team's target. I would say he really benefited from the second of the magnificent 7, which tells you to wave goodbye to any notions of achieving perfection. Think about it: his publishing environment was a breeding ground for competition and the culture was that failure at anything showed weakness. He had to learn that no matter who you are and what you do, it is okay to fail once in a while.

Diane

I met Diane, 44, in January 2009 when GMTV commissioned me to work for them as the resident Job Catcher, supporting one of the redundant employees from Woolworths. Diane had worked at Woolworths for a number of years as a line manager and was devastated when the news came that the company was going down the tubes. My first impression of Diane was that the shock of losing her job had understandably seriously damaged her confidence. The perception she had of herself was one of a second-rate product. She didn't believe she had the ability to perform well at a job interview, felt intellectually inferior and couldn't even contemplate a new employer taking her on. But I felt differently — in fact, very differently. Diane communicated with me in a way that I found stimulating and in many ways I couldn't understand why she was so hard on herself. I saw the potential and got to work on applying the 7 Secrets.

The aim was to totally turn around the negative thoughts Diane had fed her mind. I applied the secrets over a four-week period, live on GMTV, with an emphasis on letting go of the past, sorting the head out, stretch techniques and cranking up the charisma. Really getting Diane's charisma going was the key to helping her to rebuild her personal brand and hold her head up high again.

After two weeks of intensive work with me she looked glamorous and reported that the blockage to her confidence was melting. By week four, she had attained a new management role at Tesco.

Tom

Tom, 31, visited me in the middle of 2006 complaining that his confidence was low after his girlfriend of five years had left him for pastures new. Tom was a stockbroker and for the last six months he'd completely thrown himself into work. But all that had caught up on him. By focusing solely on his work, he had entered a period of denial and the experience of his girlfriend tottering off with a new man had deeply dented his self-confidence.

He complained of feeling unattractive, not worthy

and second best. The thoughts he was giving himself had become a destructive cancer that had eaten away at the core of his self-esteem. At our first session, Tom broke down. It was important that I developed an immediate action plan with him and it was apparent that all 7 Secrets needed to be worked through. Of prime importance was sorting his head out and practising exercises that would quickly give Tom the feeling and belief that his confidence was back. A quick way to do this is detailed in Mind Game 8: Automatic Trigger on page 73. It's quick and simple — you keep bringing back the times when you felt hugely confident and start to feel those emotions all the time.

We worked together over a six-week period, with the ultimate goal being that Tom's thought processes would be reversed and his confidence elevated to such a degree that he rated himself highly and perceived himself as a hot catch that could chat up any member of the opposite sex with ease. Tom worked through the secrets, and seeing him grow was personally rewarding for both of us. A few months ago I received an update from Tom informing me that he will be getting married next year and my invitation to the wedding would be in the post.

In some ways, rebuilding Tom's self-confidence was easy. The trick was getting him to put the past in the past and to see that tomorrow could bring something new and wonderful into his life. It worked a treat with Tom and I know no matter what happens to him in the future, he has the secrets under his belt to take him through it.

Your secrets

- Accept that building confidence is down to no one but you.

- Note that no one can make you feel anything.

- Take action to carry out the 7 Secrets.

- Get excited about building your confidence or it's a case of staying the way you are.

Part One

What and How

The Past is Past

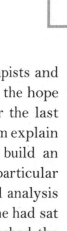

My distaste for the psychodynamic psychotherapists and counsellors who love delving into the past in the hope of helping someone move forward has increased over the last ten years. It really galls me when I hear so many of them explain that their therapeutic intervention designed to help build an individual's self-esteem can take years. I recall one particular experience when a guy calling himself a transactional analysis psychotherapist enthusiastically explained that someone had sat in his therapy chair for ten years and hadn't quite reached the point where they could move forward with their life. As far as I am concerned, that is a disgrace, a complete failure not on the part of the client but the therapist. As I recall my conversation with this so-called 'people helper', I am in many ways not surprised his client failed to move on, as I don't believe this guy could have inspired the hungry to eat a gorgeous meal at their favourite restaurant.

Why is it that many of these psychodynamic counsellors and therapists always proclaim that something back in the past is responsible for how you are today? Let's take my distaste for tomato ketchup as an example. Is that because something happened in my childhood? No! It's because I tasted it and didn't damn well like it. Simple really, isn't it? As another example, my friend Sally once described her desire to overcome a fear of spiders. She consulted a psychodynamic counsellor for three months and failed to move on. The counsellor, who in my opinion was a cardigan-wearing theorist, explained that the problem must have started when she was six years old, when a spider came out from under the bed while she was playing with her sister. Erm, well, perhaps this was the case, but all the counsellor decided to do with that piece of information was talk about it for three months. An unforgivable waste of his client's time!

Yes, you are right in thinking that I have no time for these people. No matter how much Freudian theory they wrap into their arguments, I would rather employ Santa Claus to sort out my life issues. Don't get me wrong, a little exploration into the past is fine but, please, a whole three months or, even worse, ten years! Of course they would at this point explain that my issue with this has something to do with my past. What's also a little scary is that over the years I have met several therapists or counsellors who I consider need help themselves. These people then have the cheek to be sorting out other people's lives. Thank goodness I came into contact with clinical hypnotherapy, something that not only changed my life but became my passion. It was for that reason that I decided to train and later qualify as a practitioner over ten years ago, and I have since worked with thousands of clients on a range of issues, supporting them in increasing their confidence.

> If you are an analysis junkie, then let go

But looking at in a fairer, more objective way, I acknowledge there are a few therapists and counsellors out there who do some good work. I just base my thoughts on personal experience. If you are an analysis junkie, then let go and decide that today you are going to do something practical. If you have been visiting a therapist for months on end and, in all honesty, don't feel you are moving forward, then sack them. The past really is the past and harping on about it without taking action won't help you to get back your confidence. In fact, it will have the opposite effect. Discussing past events over and over again is simply going to keep you stuck on the starting blocks when it comes to changing your life for the better and building your confidence in order to move forward. Utilise my practical tips to help let go and move on, so that you can feel better about yourself and the world around you and enjoy a brighter future. Remember, there is nothing you can do about the past but there is much you can do to shape a perfectly bright future.

Give yourself permission

If the past is affecting you in some way, I want this book to shout out at you and give you permission to let it go. You may well have struggled over the years with something that happened all those years ago, but holding on is only going to make one person suffer – and that's you. Now is the time to give yourself the permission to move on. It happened back then and there is nothing that can reverse that. I want you to mentally accept that you have the right to let it go. Nothing is going to stop your move forward to what can be a wonderful future, where you – yes, you – radiate a confidence that others can only dream of. Permission is fundamental when letting go. You are telling yourself it's time to ditch the past, it's time to move on. Tell yourself right now that you accept that you have permission to let go.

Forgive and forget

If other people were involved in events in the past that have had an effect on your confidence, forgiving them for what they did back then can be a tough call. But it's important. Some of my clients report being bullied at school – verbally put down and sometimes physically beaten. Yes, of course that will have shaped how you feel today, but letting these little dicks get the better of you now will achieve nothing for anybody. Sit and reflect on who you consider contributed to your low levels of confidence and then mentally or verbally express your forgiveness. Perhaps take a walk in the park, verbalising forgiveness in your own way, or talk to a friend and explain that you forgive those who went out of their way to put you down and hold you back. This strategy doesn't work for everyone, so if it's not for you, then choose one or two of the other strategies. My point here is to forgive yourself and those around you. If you sense some guilt from the past, let it go. It's okay and you're okay, so let it go.

Get angry and get even

Letting go of anger associated with past events that damaged your confidence is important. Anger is a completely natural human emotion and, in some contexts, it can be very helpful. It can be expressed in a variety of degrees, from mild annoyance to absolute rage. It can be very useful to release anger if you are brooding over memories of events that harmed you emotionally.

Expressing anger needs to be done with care. Anger expressed in an uncontrolled manner – physically or verbally – can result in you and others becoming emotionally or physically damaged. Equally, when anger is held in and pushed to one side, it can be destructive because small annoyances can boil up into dangerous explosions of anger. It can cause physiological and psychological problems such as hypertension, grinding of teeth, depression and psychosomatic illness. Unexpressed anger can also result in inappropriate behaviour patterns, such as passive-aggressive communication when engaging with others.

Releasing anger should be done assertively with appropriate expression in a safe environment, without hurting others. If you are living life with a serious degree of pent-up anger brought on by some a-hole in years gone by who dragged you down, then some good anger-releasing exercises will help you out.

Try placing a towel over the pillow and in the centre of it imagine what or whom you are angry about. Then get hold of a bat and, in a safe place, smash the pillow with the bat. As the bat hits the pillow, yell out the anger. That's right, yell as loud as you can, thinking all the time what it is you are angry about. However, use this technique with caution. You don't want the neighbours complaining and if you have a health condition, give this one a miss – I don't want you keeling over with over-excite-ment. Alternatives can include setting up a punch bag in the garage or going for a run in the country, yelling out the anger. If you aren't quite up to this physically, try writing down all the anger. Be as colourful as you want with your language. Forget 'em! They messed with your head, so now mess with theirs in your own safe, controlled way. Once you have released the anger, do some relaxation and accept that you have let go.

> **" Be as colourful as you want with your language "**

Other anger management strategies can include:

- Ripping up old newspapers.

- Writing or drawing your feelings and then ripping it up.

23

- Pretending to talk to the person who made you angry.

- Shouting in a safe place.

- Throwing car sponges full of water while shouting, when safe to do so.

Affirm it's gone

Once you have given yourself permission to let go of the past, it is useful to affirm for at least three weeks that you have successfully released the crap that had affected your confidence. To do this, it is a good idea to design your own little life mantra, a short, straightforward statement that reinforces your decision. This is known as affirmation and will, when repeated, firm up your decision that past is past. Examples may include:

- I am relaxed as I let go of the past.

- I am free from and at ease with past events.

- I am relaxed and free from unhealthy distant memories.

Mentally repeat these affirmations over and over again daily. I recommend you repeat them to yourself in your head 600 times a day. For example, 200 times in the shower, 200 times when having your lunch and 200 times before you go to sleep at night.

Have your say

If you really feel you need to talk with the person or people who had a detrimental effect on your past, then do so, but with caution. Tread carefully if you decide on this option. Take time to prepare what you are going to say. Never turn it into an attack or it will make things ten times worse. Consider how you are going to start the discussion. For example, simply explain that there is something that happened several years ago that you would like to calmly discuss. Explain how it made you feel but that you now appreciate that the past is past and you want to get it out into the open and move on. Be sure to listen to the response you receive and, if it falls on deaf ears, avoid expressing your anger. Instead, take deep breaths and remember their denial is simply a defence mechanism on their part. Remember it is your assertive right to have your say, so forget any thoughts you have about apologising. If, after you have had the conversation, things are healed then it is very possible to move on and continue the relationship. If, on the other hand, tensions are high and the relationship seems tender, then consider meeting again to talk things through. If you are still met with stubborn ignorance, move on and let those drains drift into the dim and distant past forever. You deserve better.

See it disappear

If you are a visual person, try out some creative visualisation to help send the message to your mind that the past is past. In a relaxed state, visualise the past drifting into the past by using an illustrative process. For example, you may visualise something that represents the past for you, maybe a shape, a still picture, or a word that you can see. See the shape, picture or word melt or evaporate. You may even bring up a past scene and visualise it drifting into the distance so you can't see it any more. Another popular technique is to take the experience from the past and visualise yourself putting it in a box, locking the box and putting the key somewhere safe.

The one-hour ritual

This is a firm favourite of mine. Clients visit me and we agree to spend one hour, no more and no less, discussing the past events that have affected their confidence. The past events are discussed and emotions are examined before a final agreement confirms that the past events are no more. My clients let them go and together we move forward, restoring, building and commanding their confidence. There is no return to the past and clients immediately turn around their mindset to optimism, enthusiasm and excitement at the thought of commanding their confidence. The hope and joy in what the future may bring is restored and the work begins.

Celebrate

Has to be done! Okay, you had some tough experiences back in the past. You have decided it's time to let them go, so you can command your confidence. My advice is: once you have made that conscious decision, go out and celebrate this move. The euphoria you experience as you celebrate will embed into your mind that you have moved on. However, I want to offer you a word of caution. Avoid excess alcohol, as this may have the opposite effect. Alcohol doesn't just give us a buzz; it can also give us a real downer. Celebrate in style and make it a memorable time, but keep it safe and constructive.

Real Life

Nadine

Nadine was a 29-year-old single parent who decided to visit me because her confidence, as she put it, 'had fallen further than the deepest pit in the ocean'. She explained that she wanted to have the confidence to date more men, feel good in the bedroom and get her career back on track. In our first confidence coaching session, Nadine explained that in her previous relationship she had been mentally abused, put down and made to feel second best. I explained to Nadine that no one had made her feel put down but herself, as that was her decision. However, I could fully understand that the treatment she had received from her previous partner had not helped. As Nadine was deeply affected by the past, I explained to her that before we could move on she had to dump the past like a depth charge into that deep ocean trench she felt she was in, and pretty damn quickly. She agreed that sitting in a chair for weeks on end reliving all the events with her previous partner was not going to serve her well.

I explained the options available to help Nadine let go of the past and she decided that she wanted firstly to give herself permission to be confident again and secondly to carry out the one-hour ritual. Within ten minutes we had enthusiastically agreed that Nadine had every right to bring her confidence back up again. We then moved on to the one-hour ritual. Nadine explained the past events in detail and sobbed throughout, at times with anger at what had truly been a disturbing relationship. Coming up to the hour, with few tears left to shed, Nadine agreed it was now time to move on. The past had sunk into the past. Over the coming weeks, Nadine's confidence increased at a rapid pace, faster than she had previously thought possible. Nadine keeps in touch and life has certainly changed. She runs her own business and has a new, as she puts it, 'horny' man in her life that dotes on her for who she is.

Mike

Mike, 34, was a newly appointed senior manager for a catering company based in Scotland. He had a good

27

business head and, on paper, looked like a solid commercial asset. Mike contacted me, explaining that he needed to increase his confidence so that he could manage some difficult personalities in his team. Prior to joining the new company, Mike had been with his previous employer since leaving school, so adjusting to change was always going to be a little difficult.

At our first session Mike explained that he was being met with hostility from a number of the junior managers he was responsible for and each time he planned to manage it, he found himself trembling with fear. He went on to explain that he was bullied at school and felt this was blocking his confidence. Mike needed to let go of the past and he decided he wanted to do the one-hour ritual combined with an ongoing affirmation that he was free from past events. After ditching the negative and bitter emotions, Mike decided that he would affirm daily that the past was past, using the affirmation 'I am free to be me.' Once the baggage is dropped, it's often like taking off several layers of clothes that disguised and subdued the real you. You will feel that it's okay to express yourself naturally, to smile at people, meet their eyes and tell others you are comfortable being you. I coached Mike for a total of five weeks, with the final session being a celebration over lunch. Mike had told his confidence to act and the past was now a far and distant memory. A year on, Mike is doing a tremendous job and is on track for promotion to be a company director.

Sasha

Sasha was a bubbly and beautiful young woman who was a professional dance teacher. She came to me because she wanted to get her confidence absolutely sky-high to nail an audition to be a dance advisor for a major TV show. The real problem was that, although she seemed to exude confidence from every pore, she had a complete block and failure of confidence when it came to auditioning in front of strangers — startling, when you consider she prepared her students to go to auditions all over the country.

At our initial meeting, Sasha told me that she couldn't bear auditions because as a teenager she'd auditioned for a production at her college in front of teaching staff and students and she'd fallen over and then froze, much to the merriment of some of the audience. Throughout her career, she had managed to avoid auditions and had used her undoubted talent to teach others, but now she really wanted the job in TV. The problem was that it was an open, competitive audition and she was petrified that she'd flop and be a laughing stock again.

Sasha proved to be a quick win. At our second session, I agreed with her that we would go through the one-hour ritual, to examine the ordeal that was blocking her confidence. I asked Sasha to imagine being back in the college hall and see the faces that were still tormenting her, and then to step out of her position on the stage and instead to go to the side and watch the audition as a spectator. She imagined the audience dressed as characters from The Wizard of Oz — her favourite movie. They were scarecrows, tin men, frightened lions and witches — it made her laugh out loud. I then asked her to play a movie in her mind that saw her storming the audition and the audience giving rapturous applause. She got the part in the college show.

Finally, we agreed that Sasha could celebrate the fact that she had left behind the experience of one bad audition in front of a load of daft characters from The Wizard of Oz. She was in perfect shape to go to her first audition in years, and I'm pleased to say that she went on to get the gig.

7 Secrets of Confidence

Your secrets

- Be cautious of the therapy types who do nothing but ramble on about the past.

- Accept that the past is past and you can break free.

- Select which strategies work best for you to help let go of the past.

- If you hear others blaming the past for the way they are, let it remind you that you are now free.

- Smile, you are free from the chains that kept dragging you backwards.

Wave Goodbye to Perfection

2

Are you one of those people who get themselves into a state because everything has got to be spot on? If so, you are one of life's perfectionists. Perfectionism is bad for your health because it leads to hyper-anxiety and often blocks originality and creative thinking. I'm not saying that we shouldn't all strive to do the best we can, but turning yourself into a complete wreck by having perfectionist tendencies is not going to achieve a good result. Holding on to a perfectionist philosophy in life could lead you to suffer from hyper-anxiety, easily driving down your confidence and contributing to poor results. The answer is to accept fallibility and, yes, failure. We all fail in life from time to time, even me! Whether you like it or not, you are human and therefore have an inbuilt fallibility, just like the rest of us. Believe me when I say no one is perfect, even if to you they project an image of perfection.

This is a message I want you to hold on to as you move forward and command your confidence. Remember, perfectionism actually stops us doing a good job because focusing on the minute details of what we are doing will make us miss the bigger picture. Constantly aiming for perfection at something will, of course, stop you from taking any enjoyment from what you are doing. Perfectionists live their lives by what I call a 'mustabation' script, telling themselves they must do this, that and the other, otherwise they will fail. Fallible people, on the other hand, accept that they will make mistakes and that's part of the learning process. They understand that when a job is to be done, they will do it to the best of their ability, and if they cock up now and again that's okay, as they will learn from it.

> **Perfectionism is bad for your health because it leads to hyper-anxiety**

Are you a perfectionist?

If you answer yes to more than six of the following questions, the answer is probably yes.

- Do you always expect a lot of yourself and other people?

- Do you have high standards that you consistently have to reach?

- Do you find it hard to forgive yourself if you fail to achieve these high standards?

- Do you find it hard to accept constructive criticism without beating yourself up?

- Do you find it difficult to accept that you will make mistakes?

- Do you find yourself overanalysing how to complete a task a lot of the time?

- Do you consider yourself to be quite a serious person?

- Do you often mentally tell yourself you haven't done something properly?

If you are a perfectionist, take immediate action to sort it. Consider the perfection-kicking strategies that I now go on to outline.

Be realistic

The airy-fairy motivational trainers that suggest everything is possible are, in my opinion, absolutely wrong. If they were to say that *most* things were possible, then I would agree. Life is about setting realistic expectations. Sure, there's nothing wrong with expectations that stretch you, but be realistic. When you set expectations for yourself, make sure you devise a structured plan to achieve them, rather than just hoping it will happen and then when it doesn't beating yourself up.

Stroke yourself

Rather than kicking yourself for what you haven't done, give yourself some praise. Look at what you have already accomplished before focusing on what else needs to be done. Each time you complete a task, make sure you mentally acknowledge what you have achieved. In other words, give yourself a stroke rather than a poke!

Accept mistakes are par for the course

Whatever you want to do or be like in life, mistakes will from time to time happen. Instead of focusing and moaning on what could have been, move on. Mistakes are inevitable. Focus on the present rather than on what's happened and leave mistakes where they belong – in the past! A couple of Hollywood actors spring to mind who made bad decisions but acknowledged their mistakes, moved on and rebuilt their careers – Rob Lowe and Robert Downey Jr.

People will always find fault

Human beings always like to find fault. Often this is through their jealousy and insecurity. You could spend hours designing someone's website, tweaking the design, the content, the layout, and someone will still come along and find fault. Remember that everyone's idea of perfection is different, so no matter how fantastic, how perfectly you do things, you will never be immune to criticism. Make sure you take this on board, so that you give yourself a break.

Permission to be fallible

You may think it is difficult to let go of a perfectionist lifestyle, but a good way to start is by giving yourself permission to be less than perfect in just a few aspects of life. It could be writing a work report and knowing that you've not been able to include a key piece of data because you couldn't access it from the web. You got it done on time, which was crucial, but it wasn't perfect – so what?

Make sure you include giving yourself permission to stop thinking of yourself as a failure when you don't meet your own high expectations.

See yourself as an individual

Stop comparing yourself to others. Sure, there is nothing wrong with observing how others perform 'out of their skins', but don't put yourself down as second best when you see them in action. Remember to do the best you can, rather than the best you think someone thinks you should do.

Ditch the procrastination game

A perfection-oriented lifestyle can lead to procrastination. If you find you keep putting off new tasks until you can do them spot on, you are letting perfectionism get in the way of finishing something. Remember project JFDI (Just Flipping Do It). You can always go back later and revise your plans if you don't like what's been done.

Welcome constructive criticism

As good as you are, there will always be room for constructive criticism. It's the way we learn, so welcome it in and let your defences down. These comments will make your work better, so see constructive criticism as an ally as opposed to an enemy. In fact, I'd advise you to go out looking for constructive criticism. If it's not forthcoming, go and ask for it from those you know will tell you the truth.

Stop being a drama queen

If you find that you are sabotaging yourself with emotional outbursts when things go wrong, learn to relax. When you stress yourself out about being less than perfect, you can make yourself completely miserable and damage your future prospects. Instead, relax, and even if things don't go to plan, they probably won't be nearly half as bad as you imagine. Just take a deep breath, remember that it's okay to get it wrong and move on!

Away with analysis

To plan and prepare is both constructive and important. However, if you go into deep analysis of each thought, step and plan you may end up not starting the task at hand and certainly not finishing it. It's okay to be theoretical to a degree, but at some point you have to get to work. Fans of *The Apprentice* will know that a mistake the teams often make is that they spend too long looking at the details of their tasks and often miss the big-picture goal that Sir Alan Sugar has set them. Perfectionists tend to overanalyse and can end up in the 'I started but never finished' camp. If you are a perfectionist who does overanalyse, set yourself time boundaries for the analysis itself and then move into action.

> I started but never finished

Cheer up!

Life isn't a joke, but that doesn't mean it can't be fun. Laugh more and you will find that you are less concerned about unhealthy perfection. If you are one of those serious, analytical types your body is probably crying out for a release of endorphins, so let them go.

Perfection motivates to a point

Of course perfection can motivate you to a point, helping to ensure you do a good job. But I call this being conscientious. The real trick is to know the difference between healthy, productive thinking and unhealthy, destructive thinking. You'll know if you're going down the destructive path when you start to pick out fine details and can't move beyond them when you set out to do something in your business or personal life. Make sure you don't cross the line, and if you find yourself doing so, stop and take a step back.

Real Life

Danny

Danny, 28, was a newly appointed store manager for a national chain. He contacted me explaining that he needed some confidence coaching to help him deliver professional and inspiring customer relations to his team and the public. He explained that each time he talked 'in public' he would feel uptight, anxious and at times so tense that he would forget what he was going to say to those around him. Danny was a very smart guy with a handsome face and he had all the basics in place — nice car, tidy image, laptop, professional stationery and excellent product knowledge. The only thing that was second best was his ability to communicate with others. As the session progressed, I soon realised that Danny was a perfectionist.

He talked about how he just had to achieve, what he 'must and must not' do, to the point of exhaustion. The perfectionist lifestyle that Danny was living was actually blocking his natural, confident relationships with other people. Danny agreed to loosen up a little, accept fallibility and reduce his over-analytical approach. He was to treat his customers and staff in a friendly and supportive manner, knowing he shouldn't worry about the odd mistakes that we all make. In short, Danny agreed to be less hard on himself. Danny is now an area manager looking after several stores and fully accepts that personal fallibility is now part of his life philosophy.

Matthew

Matthew was 21 and about to sit his final examinations at Lancaster University. I received an email from Matthew and immediately knew he was in a state. He arranged to see me and was completely stressed out at the thought of taking his finals. After calming him down a little, I helped Matthew to understand how he had chosen the life philosophy of perfection. He needed to modify his thinking and realise that there are other paths to success. He held a number of mustabation scripts in his mind, including, 'I must get a first,' 'I must not stop revising during the day or I will fail' and 'I must get a first otherwise I will be a complete failure.' Shock tactics were what was needed with Matthew, so I explained that he was acting too much like a drama queen and that there was a chance he would fail. My intervention, showing him he was building himself up for a fall, seemed to click into Matthew's thinking; he started to understand that it's okay to aim high and get close to your goal and that failure can help to make you stronger and more confident. After a couple of intense sessions, he accepted that even if he didn't get a first, he was still an intelligent guy and would probably do well in the wider world. Giving himself permission to be fallible meant that Matthew went on to revise steadily in a less pressured manner. The anxiety was at last reduced and the result came naturally — an upper second-class honours degree.

Your secrets

- Realise perfection can be bad for your health.

- Embrace fallibility in your lifestyle.

- If you hear yourself saying 'I must', stop it immediately.

- Let yourself make mistakes and learn from them.

- Jump for joy as you are free to be 'imperfect'.

Chill

3

Statistics have shown that anxiety levels among the UK population are increasing. If untreated, anxiety can have a significant impact on our lives, affecting our work, social life, relationships and health. Confidence is blocked by anxiety and as such you must learn to relax about yourself. A relaxed mind is a healthy mind; it allows your natural talents to flow and you will express your thoughts and act in a truly inspirational way. To command your confidence you will need to get rid of every bit of anxiety that has invaded your mind and body.

66 A relaxed mind is a healthy mind 99

While we all need some pressure in our lives, anxiety is an unhealthy emotion. Yes, there are people who thrive under pressure, and we all benefit from a little pressure now and then to give us the kick in the pants we sometimes need. But what happens when we are anxious? To understand this further we need to appreciate the role of the autonomic nervous system.

The autonomic nervous system

The autonomic nervous system is responsible for maintaining the body's equilibrium. It is divided into two: the sympathetic nervous system, which is responsible for action, and the parasympathetic nervous system, responsible for rest. When we are healthy, these two parts are in balance. When we are in an anxious state, the sympathetic nervous system is active and action is taken. When the state of anxiety has passed, the parasympathetic nervous system takes over and calms the body down and allows equilibrium to return. For too many people, however, the sympathetic nervous system response is far too active, resulting in damaged physical and mental health.

Anxiety kicks in when the pressure becomes too much, and in more extreme cases it really can lead to physical and psychological illnesses, such as heart disease, skin disorders, migraines and, of course, low self-esteem and confidence. Allowing anxiety to take hold of you over weeks or even months is dangerous. If you find yourself experiencing several of the following symptoms, it really is important you take action to reduce your level of anxiety and stress.

Stress warning signs and symptoms: your checklist

Cognitive symptoms
- Memory and recall problems

- Inability to concentrate

- Poor decision-making

- Focusing more on the negative

- Irrational and racing thoughts

- Increased self-doubt

- Constant worrying

Emotional symptoms

- Feeling tense and hyper

- Being snappy and short-tempered

- Feeling agitated, the inability to relax

- Feeling overwhelmed

- Sense of loneliness and isolation

- Low self-esteem and general unhappiness

Physical symptoms

- Headaches and migraines

- Diarrhoea or constipation

- Nausea, dizziness

- Chest pain, rapid heartbeat

- Psoriasis and eczema

- Irritable bowel syndrome

- Grinding teeth when sleeping

- Loss of sex drive

- Increased sweating and blushing

- Frequent colds

Behavioural symptoms

- Eating more or less

- Sleeping too much or too little

- Isolating yourself from others

- Procrastinating or neglecting responsibilities

- Using alcohol, cigarettes or drugs to relax

- Nervous habits (e.g. nail-biting, pacing)

Do remember that any of the above signs and symptoms of anxiety and stress can be related to other psychological and medical problems. If you are experiencing any of the symptoms outlined, you should visit your GP for an evaluation. Your GP will then determine whether your symptoms are anxiety- or stress-related. If they are, you really must take action. Sitting around moaning about it will achieve nothing. Of the 12 chill tips outlined in this chapter, select at least three that you can utilise to ensure stress and anxiety are under control.

Chill Tip 1: Learn to relax

Relaxation is the opposite emotion to anxiety. It is impossible to feel anxious and relaxed at the same time. In the psychobabble world it's called reciprocal inhibition. Relaxation can be learnt if you allow yourself time to get it right. The benefits of relaxation are plentiful including:

- Giving the heart a rest by slowing the heart rate.

- Reducing blood pressure.

- Slowing the rate of breathing, which reduces the need for oxygen.

- Getting rid of muscle tension.

- Increased concentration.

- More energy.

- Less anger and frustration.

- More confidence!

There are a number of relaxation techniques that can be learnt. Try some of these.

Focused breathing

Sit down, close your eyes and focus on your breathing. Start breathing slowly and deeply. Imagine that as you breathe out, you are letting go of tension and anxiety. As you breathe in, imagine you are breathing in relaxation. If you have any tension in any part of your body, let go of the tension as you breathe out. Breathing is normally an unconscious process, but you can learn to control it consciously, just by becoming aware of it. This is an easy way to change your physiological state.

Learn to centre yourself

Where you choose to centre your attention in your body will have a big effect on how you actually feel. Pay attention to your feet placed firmly on the floor. Stand tall and imagine all the tension drifting down through your body and out through the toes. Allow this process to continue for about five minutes as you continue to breathe deeply.

Float away

This is a great technique for detaching yourself from anxiety so that you calm down and get things into perspective. Lie down somewhere safe and comfortable and then imagine you are floating out of your body, up and away, eventually looking down at yourself. Float higher until you reach a height at which you are completely at ease and detached from the stress of life. You will notice that the higher up you float, the more detached you feel. Practise this one and get into the relaxed zone.

Ten-minute wonder

Find a spot where you will not be disturbed and sit in a comfortable chair, resting your hands on your thighs. Take a few deep breaths and allow your eyes to close. Pay attention to what you can see, hear and feel. Mentally count down from ten to one on every other out breath. When you get to zero, allow yourself to go to a favourite place of relaxation, somewhere you know well or somewhere you have dreamt of. Remain there for a few minutes before counting up from one to ten. At the count of ten, open your eyes, stretch and enjoy the rest of your day.

Go limp and slack

Find somewhere safe and comfortable, lie down and close your eyes. Take 12 deep breaths and slowly begin relaxing each muscle of the body. Starting from the top of your head, work through the muscle groups, including the face, neck, shoulders, stomach, thighs, calves and feet. Imagine the muscles becoming limp and slack, letting go of any unnecessary nervous tension.

Initially you may find relaxation difficult. If the concept is new to you, your natural ability to switch off and relax will take some time and work to build up. It is important to remember that relaxation is something that you cannot force; you have to allow it to happen. Relaxing will be a gradual process and at first you will probably find it easier to relax the body rather than the mind, but hang in there and the mind will ease up too. There is no right way to relax; you have to find what works for you.

Be aware that the quality of relaxation will also vary during any relaxation session. On one occasion you may find you just can't get into the relaxed state and on another you may even fall asleep! If you think it's not working for you, just stay at ease for a few minutes and then if necessary give up and have another go later. There is also no right time to relax, and again you will find what suits you and your schedule. Practise relaxation and you will soon find it much easier to manage yourself and your life. Your confidence will be elevated and, because you manage pressure more calmly, your achievements will be more frequent and of a higher order.

Chill Tip 2: Become selfish

Well, it may sound politically incorrect, but to be honest I don't really care! The PC touchy-feely lot may cringe at this statement, but there are times in life when you really do need to think of number one. Take my close friend James, who after spending his life listening to the troubles of others, pleasing other people and putting himself second found himself on anti-depressants, his confidence blown to pieces. And then there was Jodie, who after doing everything for her family and not much for herself found she was left with nothing when they went off to live in Australia. Put yourself first, at least some of the time, and you will be in a position to offer others something. How will you take charge of your own confidence if you are simply living life saluting the commands and obeying the orders of others? In short, it's just not going to happen. Being selfish occasionally doesn't mean you are being rotten to other people; it just means you're concentrating on yourself first, so that you are mentally fit for purpose and probably better able to support others when they most need it. There are three steps to becoming more selfish outlined below. Take each step in turn and enjoy being a bit of 'selfish bitch' every now and then.

- Go quiet for a while and put some healthy space between you and the family members, friends and work colleagues who have in the past been take, take and more take. If they ask why, simply explain that you are busy concentrating on A, B and C.

- Cut yourself off from all those friends who never take your calls, come to visit you or take interest in your life. Let them go immediately.

- When these people claim you have become selfish, explain that you are disappointed to hear them say that and that you are very busy. What they really mean is that you are not meeting their needs. If they care, they will ask to spend time with you and check that you are okay. If they want to win you back, make them work at it!

Chill Tip 3: Get well with a smell

When I hear the words 'complementary therapies' I become even more cynical than my usual my doubting-Thomas self. I have visions of some sandal-wearing hippy sipping lentil soup for lunch and holidaying at a monastery. However, over the last couple of years, I have opened my mind to one particular complementary or so-called 'alternative' therapy, and that's aromatherapy.

Aromatherapy uses pure essential oils to stimulate the sense of smell. Smells affect our mood and how we feel, and experts claim that we have the capability to distinguish between 10,000 different smells. Smells activate our limbic system, which is the part of the brain that controls our moods, emotions and memories. Trained aromatherapists explain that different essential oils trigger different moods, and as such they will carefully tailor the oils to be used on their clients. For example, lavender oil is often used for relaxation purposes, as it facilitates an alpha brainwave state, whereas jasmine increases beta brainwaves, which are associated with the alert state. However, I would like to add a word of caution. If you are contemplating a visit to an aroma-therapist, do make sure you visit someone who is reputable and qualified. The last thing you want is some massage specialist offering personal services! You can, of course, blend your own oils, but once again it is advisable to seek professional advice. You also need to be aware of how essential oils should be applied – for example, are they to be rubbed into the skin, burnt to release their properties or dropped on to your pillow at night? Ian John, who is a highly respected practitioner, offers a number of tailored treatment examples. Here are some of my personal favourites.

Uplifting blend

A blend with citrus oils, such as lemongrass, mandarin and grapefruit, to awaken your body and mind. Lemongrass boosts the immune system, lifts depression and is refreshing and revitalising. Mandarin is fabulous for skin tone and triggering feelings of joy and hope. Grapefruit will help to restore the mind and body and is excellent for purifying the blood.

Calming blend

A blend with soothing essential oils, such as lavender, chamomile and ylang-ylang. Lavender calms and soothes, reduces nervous tension and stress and is a good all-round oil. Chamomile calms and eases anger, irritability, restlessness and impatience. Ylang-Ylang is a deeply relaxing oil, easing fear and anxiety, and is also a powerful aphrodisiac.

Blend to relax muscles and cure aches

A blend made with analgesic oils such as black pepper, eucalyptus and peppermint to get deep into the muscles and relieve the stress and strain of those aches and pains. Black Pepper is detoxifying and relieves muscular aches, sprains and strains. Eucalyptus is an expectorant oil, clearing the respiratory system, and is also excellent for muscular pain. Peppermint is absolutely invaluable for general pain, clearing the mind, relieving fatigue and improving the digestion.

Chill Tip 4: Manage your time

Time-management skills are critical to help reduce anxiety. Time management offers many benefits to those who implement it. It is about learning to become proactive rather than reactive. For example, if you set yourself time-based goals, you will be so much more successful than simply trusting things to fate and hoping they happen to you. The key is to start strategically working towards your goals by carrying out time-based, consistent activities. On a more everyday level, you should try to prioritise tasks and avoid over-committing yourself, otherwise you will end up flatter than a toy bunny without its high-energy batteries. Be sure to use a calendar or a planner and check it before committing ·to anything new. Other time-management strategies can include having a 'to do' list and setting aside a time each day to check and respond to emails and messages, rather than being a slave to incoming information. Dealing with time-wasters is also critical. If you feel your time is being wasted, simply explain that you need to move on because you have urgent tasks to complete. Time-wasters soon get the message that you are a man or woman of action and learn to steer clear of talking about nothing.

Chill Tip 5: Feel the burn

It has been said many times before, but the benefits of exercise are invaluable when it comes to feeling calm and getting rid of anxiety and stress. We should all know by now that exercise is a great way to fight stress and heart disease, so why aren't we doing it? The simple answer is that we have become lazy.

Exercise has been proven to relax the mind and body, improve the cardiovascular system, bring in more oxygen to the brain and body, lower blood pressure and lots more. Without this relaxed, stress-free state, it's going to be difficult to feel confident about anything. Exercise is the key, my dears!

If you are one of these people who see red at the drop of a hat and get stressed by a queue-jumper, bad driver and so on, it really is time you took some decent regular exercise. Instead of seeing red, you should be seeing the sweat run down your cheeks from your brow.

When we are stressed many chemical reactions occur in the body, preparing it for the inevitable fight or flight response. In prehistoric times humans had the opportunity to burn off stress when an animal attacked, as it was a means of survival. We were able to run away or fight the threat immediately. But in today's society, most of us are spoilt and thankfully do not have to fight bears or tigers, so there is very little outlet to burn off the stress or pent-up negative emotions. Nowadays, we carry it with us, like weights around the head and neck, creating physical and emotional problems. Exercise can really help by providing an outlet for negative emotions such as worry, depression, irritability, anxiety, frustration and anger. You can kick these negative emotions into touch in numerous ways, such as whacking balls during a game of tennis (just look at Jonathan Ross – it's done wonders for him!), playing football, jogging or plain old brisk walking. Regular exercise provides the opportunity to manage the fight or flight response and helps the body to return to a balanced state quickly.

Good exercise will, of course, also improve your confidence by getting both the mind and body in shape and improving your control of their capabilities. You will be more outgoing and social because of the increased energy levels and, of course, you may lose excess weight, giving you a better self-image. Select an exercise that you enjoy and that you can do for at least

45 minutes a day, at least three times a week. Make a commitment that you will begin to be more active and stick to it, even if it's just walking. Always start gently and build up to more exercise, and if in doubt make sure you consult your GP before starting your exercise regime.

Chill Tip 6: You can't beat the retreat

If you are feeling a bit flush, why not treat yourself to some quality time out? A residential health spa really is my idea of heaven, being able to relax in pure luxury. A weekend break is fine but it can get very busy, so why not take a three-day, mid-week break, which should also be cheaper. It's a great way to unwind, de-stress and be pampered and waited on, as you walk around in your dressing gown and slippers. However, don't think you will simply sit on your backside for the duration of the stay, as there is a lot to be done. You can try out the whirlpool, enjoy some holistic therapies (have a snifter or two of the aromas we talked about earlier), learn relaxation techniques and, of course, get fit in the gym. Many health spas will also offer a range of outdoor activities, such as tennis, indoor and outdoor swimming and cycling. What's more, there's the on-the-doorstep access to a countryside setting, where these spa sites tend to be. An hour's stroll in the country before the evening meal is always a firm favourite, taking in the scenic views. While visiting a health spa is a one-off or very occasional treat for most, it is a great way of escaping the hustle and bustle of life and will give you time to chill, reflect and bring back all that lost energy.

Chill Tip 7: The calming reflex

This can act as an instant de-stressor. Follow the six steps and you will notice how much more relaxed and focused you become.

1 Close your eyes and think about what is irritating you.

2 Silently say to yourself, 'Calm mind, relaxed body. I can deal with this.'

3 Smile inwardly to yourself without using any facial muscles and then allow the smile to spread to your facial muscles.

4 Breathe in slowly to the count of five and imagine you are breathing in a relaxing feeling, colour or sound.

5 Breathe out slowly to the count of five. As you do this, imagine you are breathing out a dull feeling, colour or sound, as you release all the unnecessary nervous tension. Let the shoulders drop and notice your posture become more relaxed.

6 Finally, open your eyes and carry on with what you were doing.

Chill Tip 8: Be careful what you put in

Looking at your diet can be a useful strategy if you are finding you are tense and anxious. Consider doing the following:

- Reduce your caffeine consumption.

- Reduce your consumption of refined sugars.

- Reduce your alcohol consumption.

- Reduce your intake of fatty foods.

Chill Tip 9: Squeeze out the stress

This is a great technique for ridding yourself of stress. However, this technique must not be used if you are suffering from hypertension.

1   Sit down somewhere comfortable and close your eyes.

2   Starting with your feet, then ankles and calves, and up through the body to your neck and head, and finally to your facial muscles, tense each muscle group. Hold the tension in each group for a count of three. Then silently and mentally say the word 'relax' as you imagine seeing the word written. As you say the word 'relax', slowly breathe out and relax the tension in that particular muscle group.

3   Finally, slowly breathe in as you tense all your muscles together and hold for the count of three. Then release the tension as you slowly exhale while silently and mentally saying the word 'relax'.

Chill Tip 10: The worry box

I often work with busy company executives and they go on about the numerous worries that they face each day: the business politics, revenue figures, job security and more. They often elaborate on how the intensity of worry blocks their personal and professional performance because of the anxiety it creates. I train them to use the 'worry box'. Each morning, in relaxation, identify the individual worries you have and one by one put them into the worry box in your mind (imagine the worry box is like one of those big, black, lockable ballot boxes). Once they are all in, lock the box using a secret combination, take three deep breaths before opening your eyes and carry on with what you are to do.

It's amazing how this simple technique can allow business people who are under pressure and in danger of losing their confidence to strip away the 'issues' that can undermine them and leave them behind. I recently saw this with a communications manager who had just found out that there was going to be an impact on a communications strategy she had prepared. It was an important issue, but compared to what she was dealing with, it was small beer, and she used her black box to dump the initial stressed feeling, deal with it and focus back on the big picture as quickly as possible.

Chill Tip 11: Learn to laugh!

'We don't laugh because we're happy, we're happy because we laugh,' observed the nineteenth-century American psychologist William James. Laughter is confidence-boosting, weight-loss for the spirit, and this is one reason why it's proving so popular at social anxiety conferences.

My colleague Joe Hoare specialises in this area and is on a personal mission to ensure people start laughing more. His sense of conviction is to be admired, as he trots around the country delivering his laughter classes. And I can see why. When you laugh, no matter how you were feeling before, you feel better. Why? Besides the physical and bio-chemical benefits that laughter induces, there are two other aspects people invariably comment on.

The first is that people feel energised when they laugh. Why is this important? Energy is life, it underpins every aspect of our lives, it is an antidote to depression and apathy, and it is the basis for robust, healthy self-confidence. In Joe's laughter workshops, no matter how little energy people have to start with, they always finish with more, and they like that experience, it helps them feel good about themselves, and this is one aspect of self-confidence.

When I first met Joe I was cynical about the value of his work, but after talking with him and watching him in action, I was impressed. People's stress naturally lifts, and to see both men and women relax completely from an uptight position by learning to laugh was, I have to say, pretty awesome.

The second benefit of laughter is that people feel more present, more engaged in the process of being alive, and when combined with feeling energised, this lifts people's spirits. In Joe's laughter workshops especially, there is lots of eye contact and good-natured communication between participants. For more information, please visit www.joehoare.co.uk.

Everyone has a degree of nervousness or shyness when communicating with strangers, so when you spend time experiencing light-hearted communication with people you don't know well, sharing any awkwardness, you realise it's not just you. Laughter connects people. Victor Borge said, 'A smile is the shortest distance between two people,' and this sense of connection helps underpin your confidence.

There are self-development practices which can help you build these benefits into your daily life. One of these is morning laughter, where the first conscious thing you do in the morning, or as early as possible, is to laugh. You start with a fake laugh and keep it going until, sooner or later, it becomes a real one. It always does. This is a Hawaiian shamanistic practice and in principle is the same as starting your day with an affirmation. The only difference is that this is an experiential practice, rather than a visual or verbal one, and it works in the same way. It re-wires your brain. Like all self-development practices, it can seem strange when you first start it, but if you persevere, you will find it becomes second nature and will help to generate a sense of being able to deal with the day's challenges.

Another practice is the sustained chuckle – being able to laugh on demand. 'This I conceive to be a chemical function of humour: to change the character of our thought,' said Lin Yutang, a twentieth-century Chinese researcher and philosopher. People often think of laughter as a response to a situation, laughing because something strikes you as funny. Being able to laugh on demand and laughing in the face of adversity reverses that situation, and is a learnable self-empowering technique. The technique is similar to the breath-based meditative technique of watching your breath, but instead of just watching it, as you breathe out, you chuckle, then on two consecutive breaths, then three, and so on. Like all these practices, you need consistent application to teach yourself how to do it. Actors have to be able to do this, so it's perfectly learnable. What you've then taught yourself is the ability to change the character of your thoughts whenever you choose, and feeling in control of your life in this way generates a sense of self-empowerment and self-confidence. Give it a go and have a laugh!

Chill Tip 12: The relaxation script

Sit somewhere quiet, warm, safe and comfortable by yourself and read the following script slowly. Make sure that you pause between words where indicated. This script is designed to embed positive suggestions for relaxation in your mind. Alternatively, you may ask someone to read the script to you when you are deeply relaxed. If you choose to do this, ensure the person reading the script has a soothing voice and remember to ask them to pause where indicated.

As you sit there comfortably ... I want you to focus

on your breathing ... feel the air as you breathe in ... and as you breathe out ... allowing your eyelids to close more comfortably ... as you sit there, comfortable and warm ... you can think of a peaceful scene ... perhaps a place you have been to before ... or somewhere you have dreamt of ... it really doesn't matter ... it is your place of relaxation ...

And, feeling warm and comfortable, you can drift ... slowly drift ... to that peaceful place ... a place that is tranquil ... a place where you can let go ... let go steadily ... and relax ... feel at ease ... and ... as you sit in this place ... you can notice what you see ... what you hear ... and what you feel ... or you can just sit there, knowing you are safe in your special place of relaxation ...

As you rest in this place ... I want you to know that you can let all the muscles of your body ... rest ... heavy and tired ... heavy and tired ... relaxed ... first the muscles around your face ... let them go relaxed ... heavy and tired ... feeling smooth as they rest ... more and more relaxed ... all the muscles around your face resting ... you can allow the jaw to drop a little as you rest and relax more deeply ...

And now... the relaxation can slowly spread down through the neck and into your shoulders ... your shoulders becoming more and more heavy and tired ... more and more relaxed ... the muscles of the shoulders melting into a soothed state of relaxation ... the shoulders melting into the pleasant warmth of relaxation ... your neck and shoulders soothed ... melting comfortably ... deeply relaxed ...

The relaxation is now beginning to spread down through your arms ... and your arms are becoming ... heavier and heavier still ... as the relaxation drifts all the way through the arms ... through the forearms and down into the hands ... your arms now feeling so relaxed ... so deeply relaxed ... each finger feeling at ease ... at rest ... relaxing all the way through to the finger tips ...

And now, with your arms so deeply relaxed ... the relaxation begins to spread ... down through the trunk of your body ... through the stomach and down to the waist ... the top half of your body becoming deeper and ... deeper ... relaxed ... your body becoming more and more deeply relaxed ... and the weight of your body is supported by the seat ... as you become more and more ... heavy and tired ... heavy and tired ...

The feeling of relaxation now slowly beginning to move down through your legs ... your legs becoming heavy and tired ... the relaxation spreading down through the thighs ... as your legs are now becoming heavy and tired ... deeper and deeper relaxed ... as the relaxation spreads down through the calves to the feet ... all the way through relaxed ... the relaxation slowly moving into your feet ... into your toes ... relaxed ... deeper and deeper relaxed...

And you begin to feel drowsier and drowsier ... as your whole body becomes soothed ... rested ... calm ... at ease ... heavy and tired ... heavy and tired ... it is fine to enjoy a deep state of ... physical ... as well as mental calm ... as your mind rests ... let go of all the unnecessary nervous tension ... you sink deeper and deeper into that wonderful world of complete relaxation ... your whole body now feeling warm ... feeling deep ... deep in a wonderful state of physical as well as mental relaxation ...

(Allow a few minutes to enjoy the state of relaxation before continuing.)

And now in a few moments' time ... I will count from one to ten ... at the count of seven you will become fully alert ... and at the count of ten you will be wide awake ... any feelings of numbness or heaviness will have completely disappeared ... you will awaken feeling refreshed and optimistic, ready to continue the rest of your day ... so ready ... one ... two ... three ... waking up ... four ... five ... six ... waking up ... seven ... OPEN YOUR EYES! ... eight, nine, ten ... wide awake ... wide awake ... wide awake ...

Real Life

Amy

At 62, Amy should have been looking forward to a peaceful and relaxing retirement, but her life experience and situation had changed radically, meaning she had to stay in full-time work into her late 60s. The prospect had driven her to the edge of depression and chopped her confidence right down. Fortunately, one her friend's had read about me and my work on jobs, careers and self-confidence and sent her knocking on my door.

I met Amy and was struck by her outward appearance

— she was a graceful and well-dressed woman — but when she started to open up to me, she couldn't hold back the floods of tears. She said that she couldn't carry on in her job because she'd lost all her confidence and the fear of not being able to work was making her more and more anxious. In that first session I agreed with Amy that she had to work on a programme of relaxation techniques, starting with some basic self-hypnosis and a little aromatherapy.

The self-relaxation techniques had an immediate impact on Amy, who said that she had started to think about the extended years of working as an opportunity, rather than a burden. She could learn more and gain qualifications as part of her job and she could earn more money.

To help Amy increase her confidence even further, we also agreed that she should start to take regular exercise classes and perhaps take up a hobby that would help her to feel energised. Not a gym person, Amy plumped for swimming and also decided to take modern dance classes twice a week. Go Amy!

The end result was that Amy turned around a massive dip in her confidence and was able to smile and talk positively about the job she had to stick with.

Chris

Chris came to see me about a year after he'd parted company from his wife and two children. At 42, it had come as a major blow to him to learn that his wife of 16 years had lost interest in him and had, in fact, started to look elsewhere for a physical relationship some years earlier. The biggest impact was that he'd seen his confidence plummet, from being able to hold the attention of a room full of strangers, which he had to do for work, down to the point where he didn't want to leave the house.

We talked about what had happened in his personal life and agreed that this needed to be placed firmly in the past, but that his current anxieties and lack of confidence had to be sorted. I knew his issue was anxiety based on an irrational view that people, especially strangers, would think that he was boring.

Strange as it may seem, the way forward that we agreed was that Chris needed to get out and about and start to laugh and smile again as soon as possible. We agreed that going to laughter school for a few classes would be a great way for him to relax and understand that no matter how bad things may seem, a good laugh can lift your confidence to push through it.

It took time for Chris to start to feel his confidence coming back and he had a couple of significant setbacks, including falling flat on his face during a couple of blind dates, when his conversation dried up faster than rain in the Sahara. Chris had to learn how to be patient, take some knock-backs and keep looking forward to tomorrow with a smile on his face.

I continued to support Chris by teaching him a number of relaxation techniques to help reduce his level of anxiety further. A few months later Chris reported that his ability to interact with strangers and members of the opposite sex was much improved. He felt more relaxed and more confident.

Your secrets

- Select three actions to help you chill out and relax.

- Do one of them today, not tomorrow.

- Accept that the need to switch off and relax is not a sign of weakness.

- Look at the wrecks around you who look 60 but are in fact 40 due to excess stress. Let this motivate you to play it cool and grab some 'me time'.

- If you have friends whom you find stressful, bin them.

- Exercise can be the key for many of us to tune into the self and switch off and relax.

Sort Your Head Out

Have you ever felt like you just want to physically grab hold of your mind, take it out and give it a good clean and then pop it back in, fresh and focused? In other words, chuck out all the crap and garbage that gets stored there so that it does exactly what you direct it to do. Let me tell you, it can be done, although you don't actually have to have a lobotomy. Fifteen years of experience has taught me that clinical hypnotherapy is one of the most powerful tools in moving the mind from a negative state into a positive one.

This chapter will give you the tools to take control of your mind so that you can get rid of all the negative self-talk you currently hold on to about yourself and gradually turn this into something far more useful and rewarding. After reading this chapter, you will be in a position to carry out self-hypnosis using a number of methods, safely and constructively, so that you command your confidence to act now rather than later. But first, let's explore the two distinct parts of the mind.

Your conscious mind

Your conscious mind is represented by your current awareness. This includes your thoughts, feelings and all the here-and-now experiences you are having. In other words, you are fully alert and awake. Well, hopefully you are – if not, pinch yourself and get with the programme!

Your unconscious mind

Your unconscious mind is represented by your memories, experiences that have been forgotten and core beliefs. In other words, these memories and experiences are out of reach from your conscious awareness, but from time to time may reappear under certain circumstances.

For example, let's say you meet someone who reminds you of a cheating partner you dated several years ago. As you engage in conversation with them, it triggers the memories of the time you spent with the love rat. Although that uncomfortable experience is done and dusted and now consigned to the unconscious mind, you may find yourself in circumstances from time to time which are similar enough to trigger the negative emotions you previously felt. It can feel exactly like you are going through this negative and damaging situation all over again, even though it's probably far from the reality you are dealing with.

All of these experiences, memories and core beliefs have played their part in determining how your self-confidence shapes up. If you have an unconscious mind stuffed full of rubbish that consists of negative thoughts and experiences, it's likely that your ability to be confident will be trashed. What I'm giving you here are a number of creative techniques designed to help you tap into your unconscious mind and reconstruct and boost your self-confidence. My techniques will strengthen your mental processes, so you gradually become more and more confident, showing the world you're an ace and not a head case.

Deep into the mind

To positively direct your mind to be confident, it's important that you communicate with your unconscious mind. Your goal is to speak to the unconscious mind and instruct it to become confident. Getting deep into your mind first means you need to relax deeply, so that you bypass the conscious part of your mind. It might sound a little scary, but this means you are drifting into what is known as the light trance state, an altered state of conscious alertness. Technically speaking, relaxation will help change your brainwave pattern from a full, alert beta state to an alpha brainwave relaxed state.

> " Your goal is to speak to the unconscious mind and instruct it to become confident "

Let me give you an example of an alpha state. Driving to a destination you frequently visit, have you ever, upon arrival, realised that you cannot remember anything about the journey you have just made? You arrive thinking, 'My goodness, I am already here!' This is a common example of the alpha brainwave state. What has really happened is that you have been on relaxed autopilot while driving to the destination. Your unconscious mind has, to some degree, taken over. Don't let this panic you because, of course, if a car suddenly came out in front of you your brain would automatically switch to the beta wave state representing full conscious alertness and, fingers crossed, you'd brake in time or swerve to avoid the car in your path. Simply remember that in the alpha state you are neither awake nor asleep and if you suddenly needed to sharply concentrate, you would be able to do so immediately.

Your unconscious mind is also responsible for your heart rate and breathing rate. It knows everything about you! It is jammed to the gills with all those memories, experiences and all-important beliefs that determine how you behave at the conscious level. So, let's say that during the last five years you have mentally told yourself over and over that you are useless, under-confident, a failure and a host of other self-put-downs. It's likely that your confidence will be as flat as a pancake being run over by a steamroller.

The commands and information you have been sending to your brain have done little or nothing to spark the confidence that you desperately want. And do remember that the unconscious mind cannot distinguish between what's good and bad for you; if you tell it you are useless, it will accept you are useless. However, the flipside is brilliant news – in a deeply relaxed state you will be able to reverse all the negative claptrap you've been throwing into the unconscious and come out the other end feeling that your mind has had a full deep-clean and is gleaming with energy and positivity.

Selecting one or more of the following techniques will help you work in partnership with your unconscious mind, so that you begin to command your confidence to come alive. Many of the techniques that follow require you to utilise the relaxation technique explained on page 57. Once in relaxation, you can use these techniques to great effect and command your unconscious mind to deliver immediate confidence. Please note that you must check with your GP before carrying out any of these techniques if you are suffering from depression or epilepsy.

Mind Game 1: Command and deliver

Before you drift into relaxation, construct three positive beneficial commands that you will place deep in your unconscious mind.

For example: 'I am accelerating my confidence' or 'I suggest that from this moment forward I am more and more confident.' Once you have entered a deep state of relaxation, mentally repeat over and over again the positive commands. As you repeat these commands, imagine them sinking into the back of your mind, the unconscious mind. Once you have placed the commands into your mind, finish off by taking six deep breaths and then count up from one to ten, opening your eyes at the count of eight and feeling fully alert and wide awake at the count of ten.

Mind Game 2: The confidence room

Induce as deep a state of relaxation as possible. Then visualise in your mind walking to the door of a room. Notice the colour of the door and on it a sign with big, bold letters reading 'Confidence Room'. As you look at these words, notice how powerful they make you feel, mentally strong, proud, even excited. In your mind, walk towards the door and allow those feelings to increase. Open the door and notice you are walking into a room to be greeted by a character who you will now know as your friend of confidence. This friend is your support, your ally. In fact, you trust this friend so much that you have given him the power to turn up the dial controlling your confidence in different areas of your life. Begin speaking to your friend about confidence, with regard to where you need some extra confidence. Discuss all the ins and outs of where in particular you need the confidence you desire to make a difference to you. Your friend is there to listen and will command the confidence to act when you leave the room. Once the discussions have been completed, turn around and walk out of the room, close the door behind you and let your mind go blank. Finally, count up from one to ten, opening your eyes at the count of eight and becoming fully wide awake at the count of ten. Confidence is now under your control and it's your ally and your best friend. You are ready to enjoy the rest of the day feeling confident and proud.

Mind Game 3: Stroke the ego

Once you have gone into a deep state of relaxation, give yourself a number of positive suggestions about you and your life. Remember, only positive, beneficial suggestions will be accepted, so avoid statements such as 'I will not be hard on myself' or 'I won't think of putting myself down.' The words 'not' and 'won't' are negative and often lead us into doing the opposite of what we actually want to do. For example, say to yourself, 'I will not think of Mickey Mouse' and guess what? Yes, point made. Instead, develop suggestions such as 'I will feel much calmer as the days and weeks go by, noticing how I ooze a confidence that impresses those around me, so much so that I sell myself confidently, inspiring those around me.' Stroking the ego is absolutely fine, as long as you recognise that other people also have that right. So stroke away!

Mind Game 4: Body armour

If you feel you need to protect yourself from those who consistently try to put you down, pick fault with what you do, or simply dismiss your opinions, then start to imagine you are wearing solid body armour made of thick steel. Drift into a trance and imagine the body armour covering every part of you. Notice what colour it is, how it feels to have this protecting you and even the sound of you moving in it. Then go one step further by noticing how strong you are when others dismiss you or put you down. This body armour protects you from these petty attacks and ensures that you stand up for yourself in a totally constructive and confident way.

Mind Game 5: Fine fusion

This technique involves hypnotic regression. Spooky it may sound, but it is not, and it is very simple. Go into the deepest state of relaxation you can. Then drift back to a time when you felt really confident. Notice what you see, hear, feel, even smell and taste. Inflate that experience in your mind by making it brighter and louder, and intensify the confident feelings you had back then. Placing that positive experience to the side for a few moments, bring into your mind an area of life where you would like to really command your confidence. For example, this could be when delivering a presentation, going on a date or meeting new people, it really doesn't matter. Then drift back to the confident experience, mentally bring forward the positive, confident feelings associated with it and fuse them into the area of life that is crying out for more self-confidence. As the confident feelings fuse in, visualise yourself now exuding confidence. Carry out this fusion six times before opening your eyes, ready to continue with the rest of your day.

Mind Game 6: Soap opera

Time for drama! Has to be one of my favourites, I hear you say. Yes, you are quite right! In a deeply relaxed state, visualise yourself performing confidently and with dazzling brilliance in a situation that currently completely fazes you. See what you see, hear what you hear and feel what you feel – all completely positive, of course. In other words, be the star of your own soap opera and imagine the ratings for it are through the roof. Pay attention to the engagement you have with other people in your little soap. For example, if your soap opera is about you delivering a presentation, see the audience smiling, enjoying it and being completely engrossed in what you have to say. If, on the other hand, your soap opera is you on a first date, notice how the conversation flows naturally, how gorgeous you look and how desperate your date is to see you again and, yes, even to get you into bed if that floats your boat.

Mind Game 7: Phobia fix

You may be one of those people who feel supremely confident most of the time, but there's something – a situation, an animal even – that can turn you into wobbling jelly and a nervous wreck. This is a phobic trigger. If you have a specific situation that creates a perceived fear, it is possible to clear this fear by using what I like to call the phobia fix. If it is safe and comfortable for you to do so, follow these steps:

1   Let your mind go blank and drift into a favourite place of relaxation. Staying relaxed and secure, imagine the phobic situation.

2   Put the phobic image to one side of your mind and allow yourself to drift back to a time when you had feelings of relaxation, calm, security and tranquillity. Make this image very clear, making it brighter and turning up the sounds, feelings and even the smells, as if it were happening to you right now. Let the feelings grow and then grasp those feelings, bring them all the way forward with you and continue to experience them as you bring back the phobic situation. Let these feelings fuse into the phobic situation.

3   Repeat this sequence, but drift back to a situation when you had feelings of confidence and control. Again, bring those feelings forward and fuse them into the phobic image. Repeat this twice.

4   Repeat the sequence again, this time drifting back to a time when you were very amused and wanted to laugh,

even though you probably shouldn't. Let these feelings fuse into the phobic image. Repeat this three times.

5 Now see yourself in the future, in the phobic situation, with all these new positive feelings. Feel yourself even wanting to laugh and smile.

6 Complete the process by congratulating yourself that you are in control and have successfully moved forward. You can face your fear and keep your confidence in place.

Mind Game 8: Automatic trigger

This is a routine that doesn't require relaxation. If you are one of those people who is keen to do something quickly each day to exercise confidence then this technique may be for you. Simply sit in a seat and imagine a time when you were superbly confident. As you re-experience the confidence press your thumb on to the index finger. Do this every day for at least three weeks and it won't be long before your unconscious mind is conditioned to accept automatically that, when you squeeze your thumb and index finger that same confidence is exuded in your mind and body.

Mind Game 9: Speak for yourself

You already know by now the power of positive self-talk. This technique involves walking and talking alone in a really confident way – in other words, as if you are really confident. Always keep your language positive. For example, imagine you are giving a presentation on a topic you know well. Move your body as if you are confident, stand tall and talk as if you're inspiring the audience. You can see the fixed attention of your audience, their nods of recognition, their smiles and, finally, their applause, as you nail the presentation and people walk up to talk to you and find out more.

Practising this for a few minutes on a daily basis will automatically programme this state as a new health habit.

Mind Game 10: Acting as if . . .

Your mind needs to get used to being confident. By acting as if you are confident every day, you are sending messages to your unconscious mind that this is the way you are. When you get out of bed tomorrow, I want you to imagine you are incredibly confident (remember, confidence isn't arrogance). Think of something you have got to do that day or that week which requires confidence. It could be that you are doing something completely new, such as learning to drive a rally car. Watch how others drive a rally car and act like them. In other words, think confidence.

> ❝ Just do what confident people do ❞

You should move your body like a confident person, give yourself positive self-talk, use a confident tone and just do what confident people do. The more you act as if you are confident, the more you will become confident.

Mind Game 11: Ditching negativity

As you relax, imagine a symbol that represents negativity and begin to notice it becoming smaller and smaller. Smile to yourself as you place a silly hat on top of it. The more you are smiling and looking at it, the more amusing this funny hat becomes. Then put comic spectacles on it and imagine it riding a bike. As you look at it, see it create a silly name for itself and let this make you giggle. The more ridiculous the better! See it now as small and silly. After a couple of minutes, find a positive image of you and make it bigger, brighter and louder. Notice how proud you are of yourself and see people around you looking proud too. Feel stronger and in charge. Let that energy flow as you become more aware of your confidence.

Mind Game 12: Clear goal model

Originally developed by Michael Joseph, the clear goal model quite frankly changed my life. This three-stage model will programme your mind to unconsciously achieve your goal. In the context of confidence, the three-stage process includes:

1   *Developing the outcome.* A success mechanism always has an outcome which is conceived of as already in existence, in either actual or potential form. You are nothing without a dream, so for seven days, in relaxation, see, hear and feel the end result of you being and acting naturally confident. Of course, make sure the outcome is realistic rather than fantasy, and it's important to be self-motivated to grab hold of it.

2   *Consistent activities.* Working back from the outcome, it is important to identify all the consistent activities you carry out in order to be confident. This may include strong body language, an expressive voice tonality, a calm persona and strong self-belief. Having grasped your outcome, list the consistent activities you are carrying out that align to the outcome. Then, for the next seven days, again in relaxation, process all of those activities in your mind. Of course, as well as processing these confidence habits in your mind, you will need to practise them.

3 *Immediate tasks.* Finally, think of all the consistent activities you have listed. It is now time to turn on the ignition and carry out some of the immediate tasks. I recommend you start with three immediate tasks. For example, good eye contact, an upright posture and stating your own opinions, all critical confidence habits. For seven days, induce relaxation and focus on each of them. Once again, as well as processing them in the mind, be sure you carry them out on a practical level.

Mind Game 13: Dissociate and reintegrate

This is a great technique for training the mind to understand that you are letting go of one particular emotion or state and welcoming in another. By practising this, your mind will become conditioned over time to accept a more resourceful way of being and you will become more confident. Follow these steps:

1 Sit comfortably, with your hands on your thighs but palms turned up.

2 Creatively begin to form an image of a part of you that represents a lack of confidence in one of your hands. If you cannot see it, then feel or hear it.

3 Then form an image of a part of you that represents superb levels of confidence and see, feel or hear this in the other hand.

4 Imagine now that a negotiation, the goal being that both parts want to help increase your confidence, is taking place between the two parts, with you acting as arbitrator.

5 Once the negotiation has taken place and it is agreed that they will work together to help increase your confidence, see, hear and feel the part representing confidence becoming bigger, brighter and louder.

6 Finally, bring your hands together to form one unified image where confidence has increased dramatically and take your hands to your body and imagine that strength of confidence moving into your being.

Mind Game 14: Opening the gate to confidence

This is one of the most popular techniques I facilitate with clients. It works along the same lines as the dissociate and reintegrate technique. Key steps are as follows:

1 Sit comfortably in a chair and close your eyes. Imagine a fence is around you and pay attention to its structure, noticing how high it is, what condition it is in, perhaps how it feels and its colour.

2 Feel your breathing. Breathe in through your nose and out through your mouth.

3 See a gate in the fence, and again notice its condition, how it feels and maybe what colour it is.

4 Mentally open the gate and, as you breathe out, imagine you are letting go of everything that is blocking your confidence. As you breathe in, imagine breathing in confidence, calm and a sense of being at ease with yourself.

5 Continue this process for a few minutes.

6 Finally, affirm in your mind that this process will continue to take place automatically for the rest of the day and as you sleep. Then open your eyes and continue with what you were doing.

Mind Game 15: The confidence script

The following script is something I developed several years ago. It is designed to install positive suggestions into your mind, all for your benefit, so that your confidence can grow. To use the script, simply sit somewhere comfortable in a quiet, warm room, place your hands on your thighs, relax deeply by letting all your muscles become heavy and tired and then count down slowly from ten to one. Once you are relaxed, slowly read the script to yourself. Alternatively, you may get someone to read the script to you slowly, as you relax comfortably with your eyes closed.

If you choose to get someone to read the script, it is best to signal that you are ready to begin by simply lifting one of your index fingers rather than speaking out loud, so that your relaxation isn't disturbed. Notice that there are intervals between certain words to help ensure the script sinks deep into your mind.

Now...as you are relaxing deeper and deeper...really enjoying this depth of relaxation...feeling safe and secure as we continue...so beautifully relaxed and safe...that the unique part of you...your inner genius...your unconscious mind...is so receptive... receptive to what I say...as you continue to enjoy this special time...this special time for you...

And as I speak to your unconscious mind...that very special part of you...that knows everything about you...that part that will always support you...you will begin to exercise in a very natural way...your ability to influence the way you think about your own self-confidence...as natural as water floating down a stream...and as you do so...you will have greater influence over the way you feel...and over the way you behave...

All of these things I tell you...they will remain so positively placed deep down in the unconscious part of your mind...and continue to provide that same great influence...over your thoughts...your feelings...and your actions...just as strongly...just as naturally... just as powerfully...wherever you are...as when you are with me in this room...

You are now so deeply relaxed...so peaceful...feeling a real sense of tranquillity...so settled in your own special place...so calm and secure...so that every-thing I suggest to you that is going to happen...for your benefit...will happen exactly as I tell you...

These things that will happen...will continue to happen for your benefit every day...and you will enjoy these same feelings...every day...both inside and outside of this room ... as your mind absorbs ... these powerful and positive suggestions ... that sink deeper and deeper into your unconscious mind ...

As each day passes ... you will become so deeply at ease with yourself ... and so deeply interested in whatever you are doing ... as you relax more and more completely ... about yourself ... and what is going on around you ... feeling at ease ... deeply at ease with yourself ...

And as you feel more and more at ease with yourself ... you will focus on things that really matter ... that in turn provides large helpings of inner contentment ... inner security ... and personal self-esteem ...

So contented ... you will enjoy your own inner confidence ... the sun will shine more and more progressively ... you will enjoy a sense of personal well-being ... hearing and seeing yourself in a flourishing, positive light ...

As each day passes ... you will become stronger and steadier ... your inner mind calmer and clearer ... more composed ... more placid ... more tranquil ... a sense of confidence spreading through your whole mind and body ... giving your whole attention to whatever you are doing ... so completely focused ...

Each day you will begin to enjoy ... such positive feelings ... in a natural, calm way ... you will feel so completely settled ... both mentally and physically settled ... both inside and outside of this room ...

As you become and as you remain ... more and more

relaxed about yourself . . . so completely contented . . . you will develop a much greater depth of self-confidence . . . a natural feeling of confidence in your abilities . . . seeing yourself perform in ways never seen before . . . feeling the success as you blossom with so much self-confidence . . . feeling a sense of natural relaxation along the way . . .

And as the confidence continues to flow through your mind and body . . . you will feel more independent . . . seeing and hearing yourself exude a natural assertiveness . . . whatever things may be . . . your confident talent shining through . . .

A greater feeling of well-being will drift through your body as your confidence is now increasing . . . all with comfort and ease . . . a natural feeling of personal safety . . . and security . . . as you see and feel yourself more and more relaxed . . . than you have felt in a long, long time . . .

And these things will happen . . . exactly as I say they will happen . . . so powerfully . . . so completely . . . you will feel . . . you will see and hear yourself . . . much happier . . . much more contented . . . more optimistic in all that you do . . . as the confidence continues to sink deeper . . . and deeper into your mind and body . . .

And as the days . . . weeks . . . and months go by . . . your confidence . . . increasing as it will continue to increase . . . is helping you to release your natural talents . . . your free-flowing opinions . . . your free-flowing sense of independence . . .

Altogether ... such large helpings of self-esteem ... large helpings of self-confidence ... large helpings of contentment and relaxation ... will make it seem like ... a burden has been lifted ... allowing you to live your life ... in a much more satisfying way ... satisfying to you ...

And now in a few moments' time ... I will count from one to ten ... at the count of seven you will become fully alert ... and at the count of ten you will be wide awake ... any feelings of numbness or heaviness will have completely disappeared ... you will awaken feeling refreshed and optimistic, ready to continue the rest of your day ... so ready ... one ... two ... three ... waking up ... four ... five ... six ... waking up ... seven ... eight, nine, ten ... wide awake ... wide awake ... wide awake ...

The mind game matrix

This will help you to keep track of the mind-game techniques you've tried and record those that work the best for you.

Mind-game Technique	Worked Staightaway	Keep at It	Not for Me
Command and Deliver			
The Confidence Room			
Stroke the Ego			
Body Armour			
Fine Fusion			
Soap Opera			
Phobia Fix			
Automatic Trigger			
Speak for Yourself			
Ditching Negativity			
Clear Goal Model			
Dissociate and Reintegrate			
Opening the Gate to Confidence			
The Confidence Script			

Real Life

William

William came to see me in May 2007, just two weeks before his wedding was due to take place. He was excited about the prospect of marrying his childhood sweetheart, but he explained that he had a massive dread of delivering the groom's speech.

He let me read his speech and the content was already well structured and flowed nicely. However, William's nerves and growing anxiety meant the speech could quite easily get thrown off course, no matter how good the written content was. As we know, it's often not the words but the way in which they are delivered that can make real impact, or lack of impact. With just two weeks to go, William needed some intense confidence coaching to give him the tools with which to bolster his confidence.

From the outset, William explained that he found it difficult to relax, so the goal of the first session was to work with him on how to induce a relaxed state. William found the best technique was to imagine himself in his ideal place of relaxation, sitting on a bench in Malham, which is a beautiful spot in the Yorkshire Dales. He visited there frequently and halfway through one particular long walk, he would find a place where he would, in his own words, 'chill and let the world go by'.

In deep relaxation, I used the soap opera technique, followed by command and deliver. I guided him until he could see himself delivering the groom's speech and it going well, with the audience responding to it positively, laughing in the right places and waiting enthusiastically for the next line. We described in detail William's body language, voice tonality and the words being used. In addition, I delivered commands to William's unconscious mind, suggesting that he would be confident, focused, calm and engaging as he delivered the speech.

After three intensive sessions, William very happily said that his confidence had most definitely been driven upwards to act for him and that the speech would go well. William contacted me after his honeymoon to say it had been a job well done. His speech had gone down a storm and the audience responded with both tears and laughter. He now even felt he could stand up in front of anyone and get them on his side. Look out, Al Murray, that's all I've got to say!

Lola

Lola had read something about me in the 'pink press' and knew that I'd helped people with all kinds of life issues, including those who wanted the confidence to be true to themselves and their sexuality. At 36, she'd been married and had four kids, but found her life in tatters after her marriage broke down and her husband left home. The other issue which was dragging down her self-confidence was her own sexual awakening, when she realised that she preferred the company of women to that of men.

Guilt and what her kids might think about their mum being gay had stopped Lola from acting on her feelings and she'd felt the confidence pour out of her soul. We met and she told me that she wanted to have the bottle to be straight with her kids about being gay and to go out there and start exploring her sexuality.

I worked with Lola and told her she needed to practise the dissociate and reintegrate technique to be able to let go of the emotions and apprehension that she felt about coming to terms with being gay and telling others about her real feelings. We worked out that she'd lost a lot of confidence after a period of being bullied as a young teenager, and memories of this often came back to her when she needed to be positive and decisive. I helped Lola to imagine these moments were placed in her left hand and that in her right hand was an incidence of great confidence. This, it turned out, was when she gave birth to her fourth child — a daughter. Everything felt right for her. To achieve the dissociate and reintegrate process, Lola mixed the two piles of images and emotions and noted that it was okay and felt good to be confident.

As Lola is a big soap opera fan, I knew the soap opera mind-game technique would appeal to her — playing out how her kids positively welcomed their mum being honest with them, how she went out to date women and had fantastic experiences. The confidence gauge really started to reach peak levels and she was set to be who she should be.

I can tell you now that Lola has a new partner — Jenny — who shares her home and the affections of her kids, and she says she's never been happier or more confident before.

Your secrets

- You are what you think you are.

- Programme your unconscious mind to do what you want it to do.

- Develop confidence habits by playing mind games.

- Think about laughing in the face of fear if a phobia is crippling your confidence.

- Practise at least one mind game daily.

Brand Yourself Brilliant

5

Perception really is everything when it comes to making a confident impression upon those around you. Of course, a cranked-up self-belief will command the inner confidence, however this needs to be balanced with a physical image that inspires those around you. In other words, your goal is to manipulate the way others perceive you by developing the right outward image to match your goals and the situations you are dealing with. I refer to this as 'branding yourself brilliant'. My friend Michele Probst, a celebrity make-up artist and founder of Menaji Skincare, believes that looking good is to feel good, and to feel good is to feel confident, and feeling confident brings success. Michele evangelises about the power of image in making you feel confident and how to use it to project as though you are at the top of your game. All these elements connect, so without the right image, you can forget feeling confident. Even if that's really what you are feeling, without the right image, others may well not believe you.

You only have to look at the world of celebrity to see how important image is. I can tell you about the time when Michele worked with Barack Obama in Chicago. Barack pulled Michele

> **Looking good is to feel good, and to feel good is to feel confident**

aside after a make-up application. She had no idea what was about to unfold. The now world-leader opened his jacket and asked her to cut some stray threads off his ten-year-old tie. At the time she didn't realise she should keep them to sell on eBay! Oh yes, image really does matter.

Make your face fit

Caring for your face is critical. Research tells us that the better-looking the face, the more success comes. Taking care of your face so that you look irresistible will also make you feel so much more confident. Skin care must be a daily ritual. If you haven't started the cleanse, tone and moisturise routine, then get on board with it now. It's crucial that skin looks radiant. There are thousands of products out there to assist with skin care. My own personal favourite is the Dermalogica range, which has provided skin care confidence to me over the last couple of years. If you are in doubt, try contacting a skin-care expert who will advise as to what suits you best. Beauty guru Angela Bartlett believes there are key areas to focus on when it comes to skin care: see her website, www.angelabartlett.co.uk, for more details.

Making up

While I'm not advocating plastering the make-up on with a shovel, I do believe that make-up is something that not only women but also men should consider as we grow into a more image-conscious society. Get it right, and make-up can certainly enhance your look. Each year thousands more men are taking advantage of cover-up products and bronzer, and why not? Remember, looking good means you feel good, and feeling good helps you feel confident.

Clare Mitchell is director of Aston Mitchell, a company specialising in make-up for men. She claims that make-up for men is not the future, it's now. Clare explains that word is getting around that guys can wear anything from anti-shine powder to concealer and, of course, the infamous guyliner. Clare believes that make-up isn't just about vanity, it's more about confidence. And she has a point. Make-up can deal with issues such as scarring or skin problems which have been the cause of misery for many years. But for most of us, make-up should be about accentuating what we have in order to build confidence from within. Women have had years to get it down to a fine art, so now it's time for you men to learn.

Let's take Aston Mitchell as an example. Their sales have rocketed and are currently growing at a rate of 150 per cent a month, and at present there are no signs of it waning. In this day and age, make-up isn't just for gay men. At Aston Mitchell an amazing 50 per cent of clients are straight men who just want to look their best and customers range from teenagers to pensioners. Make-up isn't emasculating. It's a confidence booster. It can make you look healthy and feel better. Have a look at what is on offer at www.astonmitchell.co.uk.

But do remember that when it comes to make-up, less is definitely more! Aim for a subtle, polished beauty that emphasises your best bits and covers up anything you don't want to show, rather than something that screams, 'Look, I'm wearing make-up!' If you are new to make-up, the old saying 'practice makes perfect' comes into play. Applying make-up is a skill and you can't hope to master it overnight; practise over and over until you achieve the look you want. Investing in good make-up brushes will also help to give a much more professional finish.

You don't need a lot, just two or three well-chosen brushes will do. If you are not used to wearing foundation, start by mixing it with equal quantities of your chosen moisturiser. A foundation diluted with moisturiser will, in effect, give you a tinted moisturiser, which is much easier to apply than foundation and will give you a much more natural effect. Then, day by day, increase the proportion of foundation in the mix to give more coverage for your skin. Another top tip is to choose a foundation colour that exactly matches the colour of your neck. Check the foundation colour in natural daylight and if you are pale and want to add a bit of colour, do it with a bronzer, don't add it with foundation!

If in doubt, just keep it simple and go to a site like www.movingmakeup.co.uk to get to grips with the basics. That goes for you as well, guys!

Don't have a bad hair day

Changing your hairstyle and making sure your hair is in good condition is one of the most instant and effective ways of creating confidence in your appearance. Lindsey Gibson is a celebrity stylist and believes that on all the makeover assignments she has worked on, it has been the hair that has made the biggest difference. She explains that a good, neat precision cut, no matter what the length, is always noticeable, and advises that hair should be cut every 4–6 weeks. She adds that finishing and styling is often a skill people feel is beyond them, but it's important not to despair because you can ask your hairstylist for a style that you will be able to maintain at home. After all, your hairstylist wants you to look good, so will be happy to advise you. If you do feel a little lost, you can always ask for a 'hair lesson' in which you dry your own hair in front of the stylist so they can give you on-hand tips. Gibson also has wise words about colouring hair. She believes that the colouring and tinting of grey hair can take ten years off your age, but only if done well. She adds that it is strongly advisable to take advice from a stylist, who should normally offer a free consultation. Once you have colour, you should keep up the chosen procedure, whether it be highlights or a full tint, as colour needs refreshing regularly. And finally, don't think there is only one style that will suit your face. Gibson explains that this is not true and that every face shape and hair type can take an element of the present fashion, even if you are not necessarily interested in being part of the latest trend.

Do remember that hair is a partly dead fibre, hence why we can do so much to it! But it still needs to be looked after, so always use a good shampoo, conditioner and styling products, and never use straighteners without using a protector. And, of course, invest in a good hairdryer and brushes! As well as maintaining the hair on your head, it is also important to maintain, or get rid of, the hair on your face and neck. Do keep a look out for unwelcome hair under the nose, creating a moustache, and any hair that sprouts out of the nose and ears!

Style and confidence

Style plays a major part in portraying confidence. If you walk into a room knowing that your trousers are a few centimetres too short or your top is too tight and shows off your muffin top, you are not going to exude style and confidence. You will be so worried about what's wrong with your outfit that you will become fidgety and uncomfortable, leading to you trying to hide away from the crowd and thus losing your confidence. Imagine what wearing the wrong outfit every day for a whole year would do to your confidence.

Leading experts the Style Doctors have lots of great advice when it comes to personal styling, so consider a consultation, as it's a worthwhile investment. Personality plays a huge part in deciding what clothes you wear and sometimes what clothes suit you, but you also need to identify what body shape you are. This is important, as dressing in the wrong clothes for your body can lead to disastrous results. You also need to know what colours suit you, as wearing the wrong colours can lead to you looking drained, tired or just plain dull. Once you know what suits you, selecting clothes will become that much easier. Check out www.styledoctors.com for more tips.

> " Personality plays a huge part in deciding what clothes you wear "

Dressing for your audience is important. We all dress to suit our surroundings, as sometimes we are required to fit into a mould or must look professional. You may have office rules that determine what you are allowed to wear. However, too many people use this as an excuse to look drab, wearing the same things day in day out. This affects both your confidence and the way you are seen and therefore how you are treated by others. If you get up every day and put on something that is the wrong colour or shape, this will affect your confidence. If you get up in the morning and put on an outfit in the right colours and the right shape that's been accessorised and well-styled, you will feel good about yourself throughout the day. You will exude confidence just by the way you look.

The way in which you layer and accessorise your clothes plays a key part in styling. Anyone can go into a shop and buy something, but it's what you do with that item to make it look different that counts. Very rarely does any item of clothing not need anything doing to it to enhance it. Layering is as important to men as it is to women. Every wardrobe should consist of key items that can be layered to create a versatile and stylish look. Accessories can also make or break outfits. Women should always wear a necklace or something around their neck which brings out the colours in their outfits. Men can do the same with belts and scarves.

Wo-men you can style up

The main tips for men are to keep it fitted and keep it simple. Forget wearing garments two sizes too big! Wearing fitted clothes (or clothes that fit) can instantly take ten years off someone. Look for fitted shirts rather than the big, baggy shirts that we often see too many men wearing. Make sure you have key pieces in your wardrobe, such as basic t-shirts, v-neck jumpers, jeans and a smart jacket. You need a wardrobe that can be mixed and matched in lots of different ways. Make sure jeans and trousers are floor-length, as trousers that are too short create an unflattering silhouette. Boot-cut jeans tend to look good on most shapes and the darker the denim, the better, as the lighter shades tend to draw too much attention to the bottom half of the body. Try to be more adventurous with the colours that you wear. Add a splash of colour underneath your staple brown jumper.

The main tips for women are to layer and to accessorise. Well-dressed women always layer. Think about wearing a vest or camisole underneath something else, as this instantly adds depth to your outfits and allows you to add more colour into your look in an inexpensive way. Trousers should always be floor-length, as this elongates the body. A smart jacket or coat is essential – too many women throw on an old coat over a nice outfit, thus killing it! Knowing what neckline suits you is very important. Lower necklines tend to suit most shapes and they also give you the option to layer vests underneath. Jackets with low buttons tend to look good on most shapes.

95

Finishing off all outfits with necklaces and scarves can make a huge difference.

Colour confidence

It's not uncommon to be told how well you look when you are wearing certain colours. Colour analysis became popular in the eighties, but has now dropped off the radar when it comes to advice about personal appearance. That said, there are a number of colour consultants offering this interesting service. Julie Sanders is the director of the Look Good Club and an expert in colour styling. She has helped thousands increase their confidence by identifying what colours suit them best. In consultations, she is able to find the perfect colours to suit skin tone and hair colour. She explains that skin tone helps identify if someone suits winter, spring, summer or autumn colours. Her view is that once you are wearing colours that suit you, the impact your confidence makes upon others increases threefold. For more details, check out www.lookgoodclub.co.uk.

Executive tips

If you need to build a more executive look for the first time, how can you go about it? Once again, knowing your audience is very important. Know your place of work, who you'll be working with, who will be your colleagues and superiors. There are rules within some companies regarding what you're allowed to wear, but more and more places now realise that people are individuals and as long as they dress professionally, they can wear what they want. Injecting some of your personality into your professional life is very important and it can be fun and confidence-building for you. To many people, a business suit equals smart, but this isn't necessarily true.

If you're a woman who is going to be working in a male-dominated environment, you may not be able to get away with as much as you would working in a mixed or female-dominated environment. Looking smart, professional and stylish are all important. When you put on an outfit, you need to be able to forget about it, letting you concentrate on the job in hand. If you don't feel good, you will be worrying about your appearance when you should be concentrating on other things. Wearing clothes that suit your body and colouring plays an important part in creating an executive look. You want your outfit to be memorable for the right reasons. Using splashes of colour in the right places can create dazzling results for both men and women. Once you know who you are working with, you can dress accordingly. Make sure you inject your personality into the outfit and make sure your clothes are well-cut and smart.

Real Life

James

At 22 years of age, James had lost all confidence, having developed acne. He had just graduated from university with a good degree and was ready to get his first job and find a partner. I was initially contacted by James to help build his self-belief, but at our first session I recognised that the real trigger was his struggle with acne. James explained how he feared going for job interviews, going on a first date, even walking into a room of strangers, as he was self-conscious about his acne. He would feel paranoid and endure a sense of mild panic because of his perception that people were put off by his acne and didn't want to get to know him as a person. James went on to explain that if he was able to reduce the acne, he would feel much more confident *in himself. Losing the preoccupation with his acne would be a total relief. On that note, I made contact with a skin-care specialist colleague of mine who met with James and treated his acne superbly with medication and a little make-up. A few months on, James reported his confidence was on the way to recovery, but he still needed to contact me for some specific pep talks when things didn't go according to plan.*

Corrine

Corrine was a 36-year-old single mother of two. Having sadly lost her parents, she decided that her life needed to be completely turned around.

Ten years before, Corrine's partner had walked out on her, leaving her alone with two beautiful daughters. Things became worse when her parents became terminally ill. Forced to quit her job, Corrine decided to care full time for her parents. As a full-time carer and mother of two, Corrine consistently put the needs of others before her own. She would stay at home looking after her children and balance their needs with the needs of her parents. Corrine's parents passed away in 2007, and suddenly there was a gap in her life. She had time on her hands and wanted desperately to find a life for herself. But having done little socialising, no work for over ten years and having just lost her folks, Corrine's confidence was naturally pretty low. To make things worse, she felt like a complete frump. Corrine decided to invest in a complete makeover for herself. She contacted a beauty consultant and stylist and embarked on what she hoped would be a complete overhaul of her image and self-confidence. She also decided to lose two stones in weight, which she knew would immediately strengthen her self-confidence.

The decisions to look after her brand paid off, as she looked absolutely fantastic. The new approach to her wardrobe and appearance have given her the confidence-boosting shot in the arm that took her to a new level in her life.

Toby

Toby made an appointment to see me to talk about how he could get back his confidence after experiencing premature hair loss. At just 26, he'd seen his hairline recede faster than the polar ice cap and the blonde hair he had on top was thinning. Toby's issue is one that affects many guys and it can really deliver a traumatic blow to their confidence. In Toby's situation, it was a bit like Samson and Delilah — he believed his lack of hair was making him unattractive to women and he lost the power to pull them.

The main problem was that his overall image was completely off the mark — not just his hair, but also his skin, styling and clothes. I decided that he needed to see an image consultant and someone who could help him with male grooming, including a decent haircut that would get rid of the wispy, swept-over bits.

Well, the results a couple of months later when Toby came to see me were outstanding. He confidently strode into the room, his hair shaved, neat and sexy, wearing a really smart black linen suit. Wow, what a difference! He'd even put on a little bronzer and some man make-up to accentuate his brown eyes. Nice work, Toby!

7 Secrets of Confidence

Your secrets

- Make-up can make you look a million dollars if used well – that goes for you guys as well.

- Dress for success and look professional if you have to, but add details and colour to make you stand out.

- Develop a skin-care regime that works for you – your skin's an essential part of your outward package and it's easy to look after if you follow a few simple basics.

- If in doubt about your style and the colours that suit you, get some help. There are professionals, but if you can't afford them, ask a trusted friend whose style you admire.

Stretch 6

Pushing yourself beyond your fears and outside of the
security of your everyday life is both necessary and productive. There are aspects of our lives that we fear and feel
uncomfortable doing because we don't like stepping out of our
comfort zone. In this chapter you will be encouraged to think
about how to push yourself so you experience the 'ouch' factor.
When I say 'ouch', I refer to the point at which you experience a
slight fear. Your 'ouch' is that moment when fear rises, your
heart begins to pound a little and your breathing quickens.
Stretch is all about dipping into your confidence, taking a deep
breath, focusing, and plunging ahead, whether it's getting on an
aeroplane, telling someone how you feel, or letting loose on the
dance floor.

Stepping outside of this comfort zone is a key strategy to
commanding your confidence. It's no use sitting on a comfy sofa
most of the time and spending only one day utilising hypnotic
techniques to become confident; this wouldn't achieve the result.
So, yes, it's about getting off the sofa and doing something about
it. Let's take phobias for example. I always explain to my clients
that hypnosis is only half of the battle, and that taking action is
the other. When I'm working with my clients, we will generally
spend three sessions using mind-programming techniques,

followed by some tasks to stretch the confidence. For example, when someone visits me to conquer a limited confidence when it comes to public speaking, I will generally spend three sessions using clinical hypnotherapy and confidence coaching followed by an opportunity for my client to practise the art of public speaking for real.

> Your 'ouch' is that moment
> when fear rises

There are some people who benefit from throwing themselves straight into a fear-provoking situation to instantly create the 'ouch' factor. These people want to get rid of the pain of fear as quickly as possible. This can be done by experiencing the whole fear-provoking scenario or experiencing a task related to the fear-provoking scenario, which is often more constructive. In hypnotherapy we label this 'flooding the fear'. For example, take someone who struggles with meeting people confidently. The first step may be simply saying hello to complete strangers or going into a pub alone and buying a glass of wine.

Fear blocks the development of confidence and we really do have to shift it. I recall the wise words of Franklin D. Roosevelt in his first inaugural address: 'So, first of all, let me assert my firm belief that the only thing we have to fear is fear itself – nameless, unreasoning, unjustified terror, which paralyses needed efforts to convert retreat into advance.' By adopting the stretch strategy, not only will fear dissolve, but confidence will be well and truly out in front, taking the lead and making positive things happen for you.

The stretch plan

Developing a plan to stretch your confidence is very straight-forward. Follow these six steps and you will soon realise that you are capable of doing most things:

1   *List the tasks*. Begin by taking time out to reflect and identify the kinds of stretch tasks that would give you the 'ouch' factor. These don't have to be terribly dramatic, but they should be tasks that will take you out of your comfort zone and that link to areas of life where you would like to be more confident. For example, you may want to become much more socially confident, making connections with people. In this case, stretch tasks may include asking a stranger a question or even smiling at someone in a bar and asking them if you could buy them a drink. When compiling your stretch list, avoid setting tasks that may be inappropriate. For example, if you have a heart condition the last thing you want to do is set a stretch task that could trigger a heart attack! If in doubt, seek professional advice or consult your GP before carrying out the tasks. Your goal is to complete one stretch task per day, so set as many as possible.

2   *Make them time bound*. Once you have identified all the stretch tasks and written them down, place a date by each of them, noting when you will carry them out. If possible, go one step further by setting the time by which you will carry each of them out, as this will ensure you are incredibly focused. Have at least one stretch task to complete each day, so that your confidence receives a

constant boost. Daily stretch tasks will reiterate to your mind that you are becoming more confident. Once all the stretch tasks are completed, make a new list.

3   *Take the action*. A list with worthy intent is of little use if you don't take action. Each morning when you awake, take a look at the stretch task that is to be completed. Mentally visualise how well you will do it and if any doubt creeps in, affirm that you are in control and it will be done. Remind yourself of the reason for carrying out the stretch task and that the rewards that will follow will far outweigh the struggle of completing the stretch task. As you are about to carry out your stretch task, smile to yourself and get motivated. Remember the motto JFDI – Just Flipping Do It!

4   *Evaluate and review*. With the stretch task completed, think through how it went. First congratulate yourself for completing it and then identify what you did well and how it could have been even better. Avoid pushing any self-destruct buttons by telling yourself you were useless and a complete failure. If you had a go, it means only one thing: that you are going in the right direction. Some people I work with like to write down how they felt when completing a stretch task, so if that floats your boat then do it. Many people like to look back on what they have accomplished, and it acts as a great motivator. One final point is to remember to always finish on a positive note when reviewing how well you did.

5 *Affirm the belief.* With review and evaluation completed, be sure to affirm how well you did. It's important that you mentally process the stretch task so that your unconscious mind is programmed to understand that you are becoming more and more confident. Affirm this in your mind by telling yourself that you once again proved how confident you are and that your confidence is fit and well and under your control. Affirm that you are enthused, delighted and excited as the confidence builds higher and higher. Remember to keep all your affirmations positive and stated in the present tense.

6 *Celebrate and reward.* Celebration is a big part of the stretch process. Each time you complete a stretch task, celebrate by giving yourself a reward. This doesn't have to be expensive, just something that reiterates how well you've done. It may be a meal out with your partner, a nice bottle of wine, or simply a bunch of flowers.

Real Life

Gary

At the age of 33, Gary was working as a successful GP in a private practice. Highly trained, intelligent, and handsome, with a beautiful wife, on the surface he appeared to have an idyllic lifestyle. However, all was not quite as perfect as it seemed. Gary contacted me explaining that he had been invited to an important international medical conference in Madrid and he needed to boost his confidence. Since 9/11 Gary had not been able to use public transport or go to any major public gathering and had been, in his words, 'chained to staying in the UK'. Gary explained that the catastrophic events of 9/11 had left him with such fear that even the thought of booking a flight to Spain led to the heart beating faster and an increase in anxiety that brought on dizziness and a feeling that he was about to pass out. As a medic, Gary fully understood that his fight or flight reflex was being triggered each time the thought of going out in public where there would be lots of strangers passed through his mind.

Gary booked two sessions of clinical hypnotherapy with me, to help reprogramme his mind at the unconscious level. After the two sessions, I explained to Gary that he also needed to face the phobia and adopt the stretch process. The first goal I set him was to go to his local supermarket; he'd been relying on home deliveries, as he couldn't face the prospect of mingling with so many people he did not know. Just the thought of visiting a big public place like a supermarket had previously made Gary feel nauseous and out of control. As we drove to his local Sainsbury's, I affirmed how well he was doing and told him to fix this into his mind. We entered the supermarket and Gary's reaction was very emotional, but he said that although the 'ouch' factor was there, it was not as intense as he had imagined. Tears ran down Gary's face as he explained that this was the first time in nearly two years that he had stepped into a supermarket. After this, we increased Gary's stretch tasks. He agreed to visit the supermarket three more times and then to book a seat to see Pink in concert. He loved Pink and had missed a previous tour because his fear had crippled his confidence and he instead sat at home listening to her music, in floods of tears. The supermarket visits went according to plan, the last one without me in tow, and he was delighted to be getting out and about again.

When the day of the Pink concert arrived, Gary continued to stretch his confidence. Arriving at the major venue was no big deal. When he walked into the concert hall the 'ouch' factor was there, albeit in a less intense form, and he knew he was stretching his confidence. Three months later, Gary let me know that he hadn't yet been able to get on an aeroplane, but that he was building up to it. He'd scrubbed the medical conference from his diary, but set himself the goal of taking his family on a holiday to New York.

Jack

Struggling to come to terms with his sexuality, Jack came to visit me for a one-to-one stretch-your-confidence session. Jack, who was in his mid-20s, explained that he was happy to be gay but still found it difficult to come out to his friends, let alone strangers. He desperately wanted to party on the gay scene with his straight mates.

He really wanted quick results and we agreed to set about developing a stretch plan to command his confidence. Having explained the stretch strategy, Jack and I identified a number of stretch tasks, such as letting three people know he was gay and going into a shop and purchasing a copy of the Gay Times. He went away feeling more confident about coming out and ready to put the stretch plan into action.

He called to tell me that the stretch tasks were

creating a real 'ouch' factor, but that his confidence to allow others to know he was gay was becoming much stronger. Jack explained that after each stretch task he would identify how he had carried it out and learn from it, as well as affirming how well he was doing. He would also reward himself and, in his own way, celebrate his progress. As the weeks passed, Jack continued to carry out the stretch tasks, adding more and more to his confidence to be open about being gay in the process. Letting others in on the news was becoming as easy as peeling an orange. Two months later Jack called me to invite me to a party he had organised. It was one of the campest parties I had experienced and we had an absolutely brilliant time together. Jack's friends and colleagues came along and it was evident that at last Jack was at ease, not only with himself but with those around him, who he could now be open with about his sexuality. He had built his confidence to allow him to shout about his sexuality, if he wanted to, and live life as a content gay man.

Your Secrets

- You'll know you've got the right stretch when you feel the 'ouch'.

- Plan your stretches so you know what, when and how you'll stretch yourself.

- When you have completed a stretch think about how it went and note how it improved your confidence.

- Acknowledge your stretch achievements with little rewards that show you are growing in confidence and improving your ability to overcome what's getting in your way.

Copycat

7

Have you ever sat in a restaurant or outside at a cafe and noticed someone who you desperately wanted to be like? Perhaps you have watched someone perform a brilliant number on stage, listened to a public figure deliver an awesome speech or watched a top sports person dazzle with their talent. Children do the same, observing parents as they learn to survive in the world. To develop and control your confidence to act, you need to learn new behaviours and skills by copying the excellence these role models display. Copying the excellence of other people (your role models) is a strategy that can, over time, build your confidence, as you begin to understand precisely what these people do in terms of behaviours and skills and, more importantly, how they do it. You have to become a copycat.

Pick your role models carefully

To use the copycat strategy, it's important to select your role models carefully for the areas of your life that you want to boost your confidence in. For example, if you're a guy who struggles to look women in the eye because your inner thoughts betray you, pick someone you know who gets on with women and is charming and engaging, especially through eye contact. If you don't know anyone like this, look to the movies for inspiration, particularly the classics. Think Humphrey Bogart!

> **You have to become a copycat**

Of course, it is perfectly plausible to select a number of role models for a variety of behaviours and skills. Make sure that each role model really does demonstrate excellence because any perceived flaws will dent the process of playing the copycat game. Modelling excellence is based on the principle that because we all have the same neurology, if one person can do something then the rest of us can be taught to copy it and deliver it in almost the same way.

The copycat game

Once your role models are selected, it's important to ask a number of questions, so that you understand why they demonstrate such a high degree of confidence. This includes focusing on their behaviour, attitudes, beliefs and values. Once you have your role models identified, answer the following questions to help you gain a deeper understanding of their excellence. If you know your role model personally, do ask them the questions if you feel comfortable about it and it's appropriate. If, on the other hand, it's not possible to do this, answer the questions yourself.

Behaviours
- What do they do and what do they sound like when they are being confident?

- What body language do they display as they project confidence?

- What specific words do they use as they behave confidently?

- What is the reaction of other people as they behave as they do?

- Is there a particular behaviour that makes them project more confidence?

- What one thing could you copy from this person to demonstrate you behave confidently?

Attitudes

- How does their positive attitude display itself?

- How would you describe their positive attitude?

- What attitude does this person have in particular that sends out a message that they are confident and positive?

- What energy does this person display as they execute a positive attitude?

- What is the reaction of other people as this person gives off their positive attitude?

- What one thing could you copy from this person to illustrate you also have a positive attitude?

Beliefs and values

- What values seem to be important to this person?

- What inner self-talk do they have as they display confidence?

- What core beliefs have they developed to guide them to being so naturally confident?

- How do they demonstrate their core values and beliefs as they communicate confidently?

- How does their body demonstrate a healthy belief?

- What one thing could you copy to strengthen your value base and self-belief so that you demonstrate confidence?

Process excellence in your mind

Once you have assessed what it is your role model actually does that makes them worth following, it is important to reflect on their excellence so that your mind begins to process the success habits they display.

> Imagine you are wearing their clothes and become them for a moment

This is best done by inducing a deep state of relaxation and then seeing, hearing and feeling each part of their excellence drifting deeply into your unconscious mind as you become even more deeply relaxed. This can be even the smallest of things, such as the way they use their gestures, the eye contact they offer and the manner in which they stand tall. Then begin to imagine yourself taking on these success habits in the situations where you would like to be more confident. See, hear and feel yourself taking them on and as you do so mentally turn up the sound and the brightness and intensify the feelings. Do this for at least three weeks and your unconscious mind will begin to programme these as part of your own life and you will be more confident.

Put their clothes on

When you have processed your role model's excellence into your mind, next time you are in a challenging situation where you need to immediately bring your confidence into action, imagine how your role model would behave in that given scenario. Imagine you are wearing their clothes and become them for a moment and immediately you will begin to notice that you are modelling his or her style and experiencing a noticeable increase in confidence. The idea is not to clone someone; you need to adapt your role model's look and actions and make them your own. Give your own signature to the clothes you wear, how you gesticulate and the posture you have.

Real Life

Darren

Darren came to see me and explained that he wanted to increase his confidence as a 100m sprinter. He was a member of a very successful athletics club and was eager to qualify for the Olympics. His passion, enthusiasm and focus were incredible, but he wanted to increase his confidence on the starting block position and to, as he put it, 'have a confident rhythm' as the race progressed.

I worked with Darren over five weeks, affirming his self-belief, and brought in the soap opera technique to allow him to soak up the tools to learn the confidence rhythm he wanted. Darren also agreed that he would benefit from an inspirational role model, someone in the world of athletics who showed exemplary excellence and winning success. As we discussed the process of modelling, Darren suggested that Ato Boldon, a former world sprinting champion, was the person he'd like to model himself on. I worked through the behaviours, attitudes, and beliefs and values elements of modelling, and Darren was able to pinpoint a number of factors that he wanted to take from Ato Boldon during the modelling process.

Together we worked on images and sensations, from Darren putting on Ato's track shoes and shorts, to Darren feeling the calm and confident power that Ato exuded as he steamed down the 100m track.

Darren was then able to process these factors into his unconscious mind, so that he would automatically take them on when competing. He called me several months later to let me know how well the process was working, with a final comment that it was great to be putting on Ato's shorts! Darren is now a full-time professional sprinter with a career that is moving forward as rapidly as his legs will carry him.

Giselle

Like a growing number of young women, 19-year-old Giselle had a dream of becoming a recording artist. She'd built a home studio and laid down tracks that could be found on the internet.

The problem for Giselle was to transform from a 'bedroom diva' to a national 'front room' diva. To do this, she needed to get over her nerves about performing her music in front of other people. She came to me through a friend with some celebrity and music industry connections, who'd heard one of the MP3s and had subsequently met her. His concern was that she had no outward confidence or charisma to add to her music in order to give her the edge she needed to get a break. This was a real challenge, or so I thought, and one that I was dying to get stuck into.

When Giselle and I first met, it was both a pleasure and a nightmare. She played me one of her tunes on her iPhone and, wow, she sounded hot, but to look at her you'd think she'd just come from the local YWCA hostel and forgotten she had a serious appointment. She wore an oversized hoody, dirty jeans and mucky trainers. What a turn off!

Her image problem was made even worse by the personal communication problems she had. When she looked at you, it was with a nervous and fleeting glance, and her hand would go up to cover her mouth when she spoke. She had raw talent, but her lack of self-confidence was tarnishing this little diamond in the rough.

I laid down the ground rules with Giselle and discussed how she could get the inner confidence to outwardly sell her brand and match it up with her music. The simple and most effective way, we decided, was to copycat a musical artist who she was really inspired by. 'MIA,' she said, suddenly coming alive ('Who the hell's that?' I thought). We looked her up on Facebook and, wow, a girl with attitude, looks and massive talent.

I worked with Giselle on identifying MIA's BAB — behaviours, attitudes and beliefs — and copying and adapting them for herself. I asked her to watch MIA in action on her videos and interviews and to write down what made her stand out from the crowd and why she was a star. Giselle drew up a hit list of six areas that she could draw inspiration from — MIA's clothes, the words she used, the way she carried herself, the make-up, her body language and facial expressions. She'd gone copycat mad.

We didn't need to do much more, as Giselle found a new confidence in finding her style and an attitude that sparked curiosity and admiration in others. I should say that she's gone on to be offered her first professional recording contract and although it's with a small independent label, it has brought joy and even more confidence to her.

Your secrets

- Pick your role models carefully. It's no good trying to pick out the traits and mirror the confidence of George Sampson if you want to find a partner for ballroom dancing.

- Question yourself about why you have picked a particular role model/ role models. Check out their attitudes, behaviours, beliefs and values.

- Relax and transplant your role model's keys to excellence.

- When you need to drive up your confidence, pull on your role model's clothes.

Part Two

Seeing Is Believing

So in which areas of life do people want to develop their confidence? It might sound like an obvious or daft question, but I think we really need to know what's bugging Britain when it comes to being under-confident. I asked my friends and family to start with and then decided that this is such a big question, I needed some professional help.

In 2009 I commissioned YouGov, the professional research organisation, to find out in which areas people really wanted to increase their confidence. Based on a sample of 2,118 adults, the results were weighted and are representative of all British adults aged 18 plus. The public were asked, quite simply, to highlight the one area in life in which they would like to be more confident.

66 Let's get Britain confident! 99

Based on the research, part two of this book provides the tools to help readers increase confidence, specifically focusing on the areas of personal and professional development raised in the survey. Each area is addressed in detail, with the 7 Secrets of Confidence applied. Let's get Britain confident!

Confident Public Speaking

Public speaking is one of the most common fears for many people. Indeed, it can affect people to such a degree that they would rather put pins in their eyes than be in the position of having to deliver a speech in public. But the reality of the world is that at some time in many people's lives, they will be asked to deliver a formal presentation at work, a thank-you speech, team briefing or a wedding speech. Certainly if people want to become team managers, leaders or make an impact on others in a variety of areas across their lives, they will often need to speak to groups, both large and small.

The good news is that public speaking doesn't have to be stressful. Follow my key principles and play some mind games and the thought of doing a public speech or presentation will be turned around from being a complete nightmare to a satisfying and enjoyable experience.

The principles

You don't have to be perfect

Most of us have observed public speakers and thought to ourselves, 'I could never be as confident, entertaining, funny or sharp-tongued as him or her.' Well, the secret is that you don't have to be perfect to succeed and make the impact that you want to. It's not about being perfect. It may look that way, but it's not. You can be average. You can even make mistakes, dry up a little or forget some parts of your speech. It all depends on how your audience defines success and how you manage any mistakes.

You should remember that the audience doesn't expect perfection – most people will expect a human being. They know how difficult it can be to stand up in front of others to deliver a presentation – it takes confidence to just get up there. As long as you give your audience something of value, something they can take home with them, they will love it. Delivering a presentation that is full of wit, drama and entertainment is of little use if the presenter fails to offer something of substance and relevance to his or her audience. Your audience needs to walk away with something emotional, such as feeling better about themselves or gaining new information and insights that might change their own thinking and approaches to what they do. And if you do trip on your words, the audience won't actually care very much, as long as you smile to yourself and continue to offer something of value. So forget perfection; it's not what's needed.

Prepare but don't make yourself ill

We have all heard the old saying 'failing to prepare is to prepare to fail'. Preparation is, of course, important, as it helps build your confidence in terms of understanding who you will be speaking to, picking the right topic and adding the value that we discussed earlier. But don't go over the top when preparing, otherwise you can begin to worry, get caught in the perfection trap and become tangled in all the finer details that on the day may lead you to presenter paranoia.

Use the following checklist when preparing:

1 What will I wear to deliver the presentation?

2 What are the key objectives of the presentation?

3 Does the presentation have a clear beginning, middle and end?

4 What key points do I want to get over at the beginning, middle and end?

5 What final statement will I use to round off my presentation?

6 What performance-anxiety techniques can I use?

Preparation should also include rehearsal, if possible at the venue where you will be delivering your speech. If you can't manage this, start by practising in front of a mirror and then take it up a level and run through your speech with someone you know and trust and ask them for their constructive feedback.

Don't think of yourself as a public speaker

Bonkers as this may sound, the best way to succeed is to not consider yourself a public speaker on the day you actually need to speak. Take away the notion that it's you standing up and speaking to a load of people who you might not know or might be afraid of coming across like a muppet in front of. The reason for this is that we often have a misguided and exaggerated view of what it is that public speakers do. It's then too easy to assume that to be a successful public speaker we should strive hard to deliver certain idealistic qualities we don't have. Of course, what then follows is a personal struggle, as we desperately strive to emulate the characteristics of other public speakers.

Yes, modelling their behaviour is, of course, a positive thing to do, but trying to be 100 per cent like them is dangerous. Most successful public speakers will naturally have their own role models, but they don't try to exactly copy others. What they do, in fact, is be themselves in front of other people.

The key, therefore, is to be true to yourself, while taking on board some tips from the experts. Give yourself permission to be you in the presence of others. That way you will make much better contact with your audience and keep the presentation or public speech alive. By being yourself in front of others you will be able to stand up and make a speech without any idea of how you are going to get across your points. The reason is simple. Because you are relaxed about yourself, you are able to communicate clearly and use body language freely. If you find yourself in a situation where you are asked to say a few words in front of a group, the key is to have three key points and to just be yourself. The more relaxed you are, the more spontaneous your speech will be. So forget being the consummate public speaker – be yourself instead!

Be humble and humorous

Humility and humour go a long way to helping your presentations or talks being enjoyable and entertaining for your audience. Of course, humour has to be appropriate, your audience has to feel comfortable with it – remember that even if you think it's the funniest thing in the world, others may be offended.

Humility is about standing up in front of others and sharing some of your own insecurities, weaknesses and mistakes. When you are not afraid to admit your own weaknesses, you create a safe, more intimate climate for your audience. Humility will make you more credible and believable and, in my experience, more respected. People will connect with you more easily and you will become part of the audience, as opposed to someone who is the expert on the other side. Your humility will set a tone of honesty and portray that you are comfortable with who you are.

Try combining humour and humility. It could be telling a story about when you did something and it didn't quite work out. I was once booked to give a motivational talk at a sports college and ended up in front of a Women in Business crowd. I kept my cool, told them I could imagine them all clad in lycra, going for gold in a sprint to get out of the door, and explained who I should have been talking to – it went down a treat, and I had them eating out of my hand.

Sharing your own failings to demonstrate a point you are trying to make can be both entertaining and massively illuminating. I recall a time when I suddenly and unexpectedly became nervous in the middle of a presentation. I didn't hide the fact because, let's face it, the audience can usually tell anyway. Instead I acknowledged the fact, cracked an aside along the lines of who wouldn't be nervous talking about that, smiled, collected my thoughts and ploughed on.

Bad things never happen

Often people get themselves into a blind panic about public speaking because they think that something awful is going to happen to them. Common thoughts include worrying about drying up, the audience being bored or hating them, even fainting! Yes, it would be a bit embarrassing if these things did happen, but the good news is they rarely do. Let's face it, public speaking isn't about dealing with a life-threatening situation. You may think you are going to die on your feet, but if you follow my simple advice, I know that you won't.

The key rule to remember is that everything that happens to you when delivering a speech or a presentation can be used to your advantage. If, for example, the audience seems bored when you are delivering an informal presentation, simply stopping and asking them honestly and calmly if this is what they expected can score you points. Again, it is about you showing a degree of humility. This isn't you being submissive; it is you being assertive and confident enough in your own skin to deal with the situation then and there.

> Let's face it, public speaking isn't about dealing with a life-threatening situation

Remember that the audience wants you to be hot

My final principle is to know and appreciate that your audience, in the main, wants you to succeed. Again, remember that, more often than not, your audience is also terrified of public speaking and presenting. The vast majority of them will feel for you, admire you and be on your side, no matter what happens. Most audiences will forgive you for falling over your own tongue and while it might seem a big deal to you, it really isn't to them as long as you get back on track and are enjoying what you are doing. This is an important point to remember, especially if you think that your presentation hasn't gone too well.

Manage performance anxiety

Playing a few mind games will certainly help to reduce your levels of performance anxiety. There are three mind games in particular that I recommend. Try using each and see which suits you best.

1   Draw up a picture in your mind of your confidence room, the place where you feel supremely confident. Now walk into your confidence room and turn up the level of confidence. Keep practising this and use the technique a minute or two before the presentation or public speech. It will inject a real confidence boost.

2   Use the soap opera technique. Drift deep into relaxation and play the movie of success! See, feel and hear yourself performing with confidence and strength. Pay attention also to the reaction of the audience, as you see them breaking out in smiles, looking attentive and applauding you loudly.

3   Set up an automatic trigger that you can call on at any time before, during and after the presentation. Have a word or image in your mind that you automatically pull out when you feel your confidence slipping and it will boost your confidence.

Public Speaking: the script

Relax yourself comfortably and safely in a warm room. Then slowly read the following script which is designed to embed positive suggestions into your mind for public speaking. Alternatively, ask someone to read the script to you once you have relaxed. Indicate that you are relaxed and ready to begin by lifting one of your index fingers. This script will put into place positive suggestions in your mind which will help you deliver a high-impact presentation and fill you with confidence. Remember, the script should be read slowly, with pauses between words where indicated.

As you sit there ... deeply relaxed ... you can allow your mind to drift anywhere you like ... and as you drift ... you will go even deeper ... and deeper into a wonderful, calm state of both physical and mental relaxation ... and I am ... all for your benefit ... going to explain just how .. how you will deliver a successful present-ation ... a presentation that has natural impact ... as you allow your natural talents ... and confidence ... to flow freely and easily ... as you deliver the presentation calmly ... being yourself ... completely at ease with yourself ...

I want you to know that ... as soon as you enter the room where you will deliver the presentation ... you feel calm ... rested ... relaxed ... and pleased as you see people ... your audience on your side ... a feeling of calm yet curious excitement ... fills your body ... you notice how positive you feel ... enthused to deliver the present-ation ... calm and at ease ... and you begin to notice how confident you are feeling ... how confident you feel to deliver the presentation... sure in the knowledge that you feel at ease with yourself and those around you...

As you are called to do the presentation... you immediately feel a sense of calm and focus... a calm focus as you feel completely in control... and as soon as you stand and face the audience... you smile... relax... and engage the audience with your open posture... as you begin your presentation... you calmly yet directly begin to speak... clearly... calmly... enthused as you know just how good you feel about yourself... and how glad the audience is to have you delivering the presentation...

You continue to deliver your presentation calmly... using open gestures... a steady and perfect pace... smiling... pausing... with engaging eye contact with all of your audience... and you just know... know exactly how well the audience are responding to you... all done in such a natural way... knowing how well you are doing, you feel more and more confident... confidence deeply affirmed within you... large helpings of confidence... self-esteem... calm... as you deliver the presentation with such ease... forgetting about any disabling thoughts... just thinking how well you are doing... and how well your audience is reacting...

These things I say to you now embed deeper and deeper into your mind... buried deep into your unconscious mind... these things I say are now part of you... and when you become fully alert... you will feel calm... confident... optimistic... sure in the knowledge that you will deliver presentations... confidently... calmly...

confidently ... calmly ... confidently ... and now, when you are ready, bring yourself around knowing that any feelings of heaviness will have disappeared ...

Real Life

Barry

No matter how senior someone is in business, it would seem many struggle with public speaking. As the MD of a large haulage company, Barry couldn't afford to be nervous when making presentations. Having avoided them for many years, Barry visited me in the hope that he would be able to deliver a motivational presentation at the company's annual conference. Barry explained that the thought of delivering a presentation felt worse than having his teeth pulled out without anaesthetic. Over the two sessions we spent together, Barry and I applied clinical hypnotherapy and confidence coaching to affirm belief in Barry's ability to deliver a presentation.

Barry also began to accept that he could show humility when delivering his presentation, explaining to the audience that of all his responsibilities, presenting was the one he most dreaded, but he had reason to present today with enthusiasm because of such fantastic company results. At first Barry felt that he had to perform, in his words, like 'a proper business speaker' and speak with flowing authority. He was, quite simply, trying too hard to be a public speaker when he didn't need to be one. It was like giving Barry water after he'd been stranded in the desert for a month when the penny finally dropped that he didn't have to be perfect. In addition to confidence coaching, I administered some mind games using clinical hypnotherapy. Primarily, I used the soap opera and phobia fix, which Barry lapped up. He especially liked the tip of looking at his audience and, just for a moment, imagining that they were sitting there in their underwear, more exposed than he was.

Reprogramming Barry's thoughts and hypnotising his mind certainly did the trick. The conference went really well, with just a few slight hiccups. Barry told me afterwards that he felt as though his confidence had been cranked up and the delivery of the presentation was a pleasure rather than a chore.

Janine

As an IT specialist, Janine was rarely asked to deliver presentations. However, things changed when she was appointed IT project leader to implement a new business system throughout the organisation where she worked. Her new boss explained that she would be required to attend the executive management team meetings and deliver a presentation each month.

While Janine was very capable of managing the project, the thought of delivering a presentation to the senior team filled her with dread. She had full comprehension of how to design the presentation, but little confidence when it came to standing up in front of the senior team. She attended a couple of sessions with me in which we both agreed that we were determined to help her grow immediate confidence and change her perception of presenting.

During the confidence-building sessions, I recognised that Janine was unconsciously coming to the very immediate and untrue conclusion that the audience was against her. She always therefore pushed the flight button on her fight or flight defence mechanism to protect herself from the perceived emotional harm. As our session progressed, Janine gradually understood and accepted that the audience was actually on her side. During clinical hypnosis, she affirmed her self-belief and utilised the fine fusion technique. Outside of our sessions, Janine continued to practise relaxation and used the fine fusion technique to mentally transfer confidence into future presentations. Three months on, Janine contacted me to let me know that her perspective on presenting had changed. Not only was she now perceiving the audience on her side, she was also much calmer and more confident and was looking forward to impressing them and being thanked for what she was doing.

Your secrets

- Be yourself. Accept tips on public speaking, but don't try to be a public speaker you admire.

- Do simple preparation and make sure you don't get bogged down in the detail.

- Know that the audience wants you to be human and natural – you can make mistakes and get away with it!

- Don't let the ego land in front of everyone – give them some humour and humility instead.

- Manage any natural anxiety with my mind-over-body tips which will make sure you don't become paralysed with fear.

Confident at Work

The YouGov survey identified a number of key areas within the world of work in which Brits wanted to increase their confidence. Not only was confidence at job interviews highlighted, but also job security and being assertive at work.

Your confident at work *check list*

- Do you bounce out of bed and relish the challenge of each working day?
- Have you set yourself a set of short-, medium- and long-term goals for your job?
- Have you recently volunteered any ideas or plans to take the business or a project forward?
- Have an honest look at your strengths and weaknesses and see if you could benefit from training.
- Are you comfortable in your role – is it too demanding or not demanding enough?
- Do your colleagues appreciate you?

Be confident your job is secure

We live in times when job security is on the minds of most people. We have learnt the hard way that we can't take our jobs for granted. Not only can it be difficult getting the job of your dreams, but equally it can be a struggle to hold on to it. Everyone has bills to pay, and our basic human instinct is to survive and provide for those who depend on us. This means that clinging on to the sources of our income is critical.

There are ways we can build up our immunity to getting fired. Here are my tips, so that you can be confident about holding on to your job:

- The first tip is about developing relationships. Make sure that your relationship with your line manager is in tip-top shape, but also develop strong relationships with other key stakeholders in your organisation. Do this by going out of your way to support their needs. Of course, don't become a doormat, but let it be seen and heard that you are always co-operative, supportive and willing to take things on.

- Secondly, be the first to volunteer to work on projects and let it be seen that you believe in your company, its goals and its philosophy. Senior business leaders want people who are committed to their vision; trouble-makers and those who flatly refuse to play the game are usually removed and depart quietly through the back door and never return through the front. Even if you disagree with the intentions of your employer, remember to play the game.

- Thirdly, make sure that you are well-skilled, qualified and a scarce product in your own right. Employers want to hold on to skilled employees, so learn a few new skills every year and, if possible, gain a recognised qualification that is directly relevant to your work.

- Fourthly, always attend corporate functions. Even if you find these events a strain, make sure your face is seen. Don't be the one who always avoids the company Christmas party. And be sure to offer to buy 'important' people a drink at the bar.

- Finally, show your ambition carefully. Don't be seen as someone who may threaten the boss because you are so good at what you do. Instead, let it be known that you are keen to get on simply because you love the business, its service or product and you see a long-term career there with you progressing with your abilities and ambition.

> There are ways we can build up our immunity to getting fired

Be confident in your abilities

There can be a variety of reasons why employees feel under-confident in their own abilities at work. It may be because of a past experience which has dented confidence, a bullying boss that puts them down consistently or that the skills are there but the self-belief to deploy them effectively isn't.

If you have suffered from a setback, it really is important to let go and move on. To wallow in self-pity and wonder why it happened to you is not really going to help you, your employer or, most importantly, your future. Sit back and realise that whatever happened is in the past. There is nothing you can do about it except learn from it. Remember that you are not alone. Everyone has setbacks at work and, strangely, it can be one of the best ways to learn. Use one of the techniques outlined in chapter 1 to help you to let go after you have taken stock of what's happened, reflected on what you did or could have done and learnt from it. Remember, you do have the skills and you were appointed for your talent, so be proud in that knowledge.

If your confidence keeps getting knocked to the canvas by a bullying boss, first remember that it is often because of their own lack of confidence that they have to put you down. Learn to be assertive by standing up for yourself in a calm, controlled way, but never meet aggression with aggression because you will, more than likely, come off worst. Make sure you take time to listen and show empathy before expressing how you feel.

Being seen as a pushover gives a bully permission to intimidate you even more, so it's important to assert yourself. To help with this, practise some of the mind games outlined in chapter 4. Insecure bosses sadly do often need to prove their leadership by bullying or stamping their feet, so stroke their egos, but don't become a weak kitten. Remember that you do have the ability, so take no notice of the demon you work for. If things get worse and the put-downs continue, ask for a sit-down with your boss and explain what you observe and what you want to happen. If this fails to resolve things, ask to speak to someone more senior. Remember, people who have skills and talents often trigger jealousy in other insecure people, who in return will want to put them down. It's not you, it's them.

Having the will and confidence to big up your self-belief is my next crucial message. It's okay to question your abilities to see how you can improve them, but self-sabotage by dropping negative hand grenades into your mind with loser talk has to stop. Just look at what you can do at the moment and see the great things you deliver, and then boost your belief by practising a selection of mind games.

Do remember that life and work are all about learning, and we all have to learn in order to develop as people. It's okay to ask for help. Is worrying about your ability going to add value to what you do? No. In that case, calmly plan out what you can do to improve your abilities. Feeling sorry for yourself will achieve nothing, whereas taking action will.

Be confident in job interviews

Job interviews can often be an anxiety-provoking experiences. There are three rules for successful job interviews.

- **A** is for attitude. It is important that you approach the job interview feeling really positive about yourself and the job itself. Not only that, but be positive about the interview experience and the person conducting the interview. Your attitude is your choice, so on the day of the interview make sure you get into the confidence zone. Make sure to practise some mind games and always brand yourself as a high-quality, exclusive product. Remember, you are a product in your own right and your attitude will be represented by how you present yourself. You have got to think positive.

- **B** is for your behaviour at the interview. Confident behaviour is about ensuring you have great eye contact, an upright, tall posture, open gestures and a firm handshake. A few days before the interview, use the soap opera mind game so that your unconscious mind is pre-programmed for confident body language. Follow on from this by using the command and deliver mind game, as this will ensure you are strongly affirmed to do well. Try to copycat by watching celebrities on TV, noting how they hold themselves confidently and answer questions. It's important to relax for the interview, so practise some chill tips in partnership with the mind games.

- **C** is for capability. Interviewers are looking for evidence of your capability to perform the job. Be sure to check your CV before the interview so you know what is on it, and do practise answering some typical interview questions so you can show that you are confident of your capabilities. Remember to answer questions giving concrete examples rather than vague, waffly answers that do nothing to justify your competence.

For more information on how to be confident and successful at job interviews, check out one of my other titles, *Change Your Life – Grab That Job*.

Be confident to fit in

When joining a new company or moving to a new department, often people find they experience a confidence blip when it comes to fitting in and being accepted. The simple rule is don't be shy! We are often shy when we focus on ourselves too much in terms of our fears and insecurities. Set your mind up to fit in by playing some mind games. Fitting in, like many things, is a self-fulfilling prophecy. If you think it will be tough, it will be. When you join a new team, the secret is to find common ground and show a genuine interest in other people. Use people's names, so it makes the conversation more personal and intimate, and, of course, never underestimate the power of a smile; it makes you more approachable and speaks volumes.

> ❝ The simple rule is don't be shy! ❞

Confident for promotion

If you are ambitious and are looking for promotion, there's a good chance that you feel confident about yourself and your capabilities. If you can ratchet up your confidence even more, promotion opportunities will be more readily available. There are a number of tactics and tips you can take on board to help boost your confidence to climb the career ladder.

Start by focusing on your skills. You have certain skills that you have developed on your own over the years, so focus on them to help boost your confidence. Write them down, as some of your skills may not immediately come to you and this will focus your thoughts. The more skills you recognise in yourself, the more confident you will come across. Of course, also know your development needs and work on them to eliminate any skill deficiencies.

Secondly, record your achievements in the form of a continuing professional development log. Appreciating all your achievements, no matter how small, is important. Logging your achievements will be a great way to recall them and boost your confidence as you look at just how much you have done. Consider also noting words of praise and encouragement from your boss and when you are losing confidence, read them through and take encouragement from them. A useful model to use for steering your promotion at work is the clear goal model (see page 75). This will help focus your mind and install the activities you need to take to attain the next step on the career ladder.

Remember that your own brand is crucial if you are ambitious and want to move up the ranks. Show your confidence by maintaining a positive attitude and branding yourself as a high-quality, stand-out-from-the-crowd individual.

Confident at work: the script

The following script is designed to install positive suggestions into your mind, so that your confidence at work will increase. To use the script, simply sit comfortably in a quiet, warm room, place your hands on your thighs, relax deeply by letting all your muscles become heavy and tired and then count down slowly from ten to one. Once you are relaxed, slowly read the script to yourself. Alternatively, you may get someone to read the script to you slowly, as you relax comfortably with your eyes closed. If you choose to do this, it is best to signal that you are ready to begin by lifting one of your index fingers rather than speaking out loud yourself, so that your relaxation isn't disturbed. Notice that there are intervals between certain words, to help ensure the script sinks deeply into your mind.

And as you relax ... letting go of all the unnecessary nervous tension ... you can begin to allow yourself to focus ... on what I say to you ... the things I say to you are all for your benefit ... as the things I say to you ... drift deeper and deeper into your unconscious mind ... and all the things I suggest to you ... to help you feel confident in your work ... become a firm part of you ...

And as we continue ... you relax even more completely ... knowing that you will become more and more at ease with yourself ... more at ease with yourself at work ... because you are becoming more and more confident in yourself at work ... confident about your abilities at work ... knowing that you are unique and that your confidence in your abilities ... is becoming stronger ... more natural ... because you are at ease with yourself ...

You will notice over the forthcoming weeks and months ... that you will be less concerned about your abilities at work ... as your abilities will naturally flow ... more naturally ... more steadily ... more comfortably ... you will also be proud of yourself ... knowing that you are confident ... feeling more confident ... as you are assertive ... standing up for yourself at work ... in a calm ... contained ... and relaxed manner ...

You will respect yourself more and more ... meaning that you are also respected by those around you at work ... they will look upon you with respect ... as you present yourself calmly and assertively ... as soon as ... you need to be assertive you will ... relax ... feel at ease with yourself ... listen first before responding to others ... and as you respond ... you will show empathy and then state what it is you want to say ...

As you communicate assertively ... you stand or sit up straight ... offer natural eye contact ... with whoever you are speaking to ... and project yourself as calm and focused ... you are assertive rather than aggressive ... if interrupted, you explain you would like to finish what it is you are saying ... calmly and comfortably ... as you are at ease with yourself ... feeling relaxed ... at ease ...

And ... as your confidence increases more naturally ... you remember to be co-operative at work ... you stand out at work ... you will project yourself positively ... so positively that you will be known as an asset ... someone who is readily there to help ... someone who is company-focused ... someone who is at ease ... someone who shines ... and ... because your confidence is now increasing . . . both inside and outside of this room . . . your potential is growing . . . you are promoting yourself constructively . . . confidently . . .

You promote yourself . . . your abilities . . . your talents . . . your confidence will continue to grow more and more as you are at ease with yourself at work . . . as soon as you are at work your confidence is strong . . . your unconscious mind is programmed to support you at work . . . support your confidence . . . so much so that you believe in your job security at work . . . you believe in your abilities . . . your free-flowing talents . . . your ability to promote yourself at work and in job interviews . . .

And these things I say to you . . . are drifting ever deeper and deeper into your unconscious mind . . . and will continue to be a part of you . . . your confidence at work is now stronger . . . each day . . . your confidence at work will increase as you become more at ease with yourself at work . . . those around you at work . . . as your talent is released . . . your abilities are released . . . your true potential is released . . . and your confidence is released . . . so much so that . . . life becomes more satisfying . . . satisfying for you . . .

Real Life

Sandy

Sandy was a 34-year-old chartered accountant who came to see me to find some extra confidence to support her career progress, as she felt blocked in the role she was in.

On a technical level she was very talented, but her confidence was struggling to take her forward and upward in her career. The big problem was that she had a low opinion of herself and constantly compared herself to others and put herself down.

In our first session, I recognised that it was important for Sandy to acknowledge that she had a unique talent and to affirm her self-belief by using the command and deliver technique, utilising hypnotherapy. We then progressed on to the clear goal model and Sandy identified the clear outcome, the consistent activities to get her there and the immediate tasks she had to get on with. As well as getting her to write this out, I embedded this into Sandy's unconscious mind.

Sandy also had a rather conservative image, so we agreed that she would dress in a slightly more modern style and I pointed her in the right direction to get some valuable style advice. Finally, I wanted Sandy to identify a role model, someone she could learn from, and apply the copycat principle to bolster elements of her own self-confidence. She explained that one of the directors at work inspired her and went on to say that her selected role model communicated with an assertive style that commanded respect, but didn't leave others feeling bullied. Sandy agreed she would practise the copycat technique to help boost her presence and confidence.

Two years on, Sandy is now group accountant for a large hotel business and is enjoying a career with bright prospects.

Laura

At 38, Laura had established herself as a successful solicitor, specialising in property conveyancing. The housing crash was on the horizon as a result of the credit crunch, and Laura had naturally become pretty insecure about her future employment prospects. It had started to eat away at her once sky-high optimism and confidence.

With a mortgage of her own to pay and a raft of regular bills, Laura became very stressed and decided to visit me to support her flagging and sagging confidence. I decided to combine confidence-boosting techniques and clinical hypnotherapy to rebuild Laura's confidence.

I taught Laura how to use relaxation techniques to induce a hypnotic trance and utilise a number of mind games, including command and deliver and dissociate and reintegrate, to help alleviate the evident anxiety.

Laura also ensured she developed strong relationships with the partners of the practice and agreed to take on additional projects to support the business's stability. She also agreed to train in additional areas and, having formed close relationships with senior partners, it was decided to fund Laura to train to qualify as an employment lawyer.

Laura was one of the lucky ones who survived redundancy during the height of the credit crunch by taking proactive action. She thought hard about how she could add value to her firm and showed confidence in her own position and abilities by suggesting she add new strings to her bow that could help win new business. The learning point here is that taking action early can create long-term job security and make yourself recession-proof.

7 Secrets of Confidence

- Be confident in the face of change at work – it's inevitable – and try to keep ahead of the game, making sure you pick up new skills.

- Interviews turn into job offers when you are confident of your abilities, and this makes you shine.

- Making a new start is so much easier when you know what to expect and have the confidence to form new work relationships.

- Work bullies will back off and change their ways if you deal with them in a confident and controlled way.

Confident Dating and Relationships

On the one hand, we love to date, but on the other, we feel nervous and anxious about rejection. Confidence is king in the dating game; without it you'll be Billy No Mates, sharing the bed with teddy bears and stuffed rabbits. The only pussy that's likely to get stroked is your aunt's pet kitty.

In this chapter I set down the key strategies to build confidence so that you can date whoever you want to date. I will also outline how to be confident when you have found the man or woman of your dreams, so that you not only hold on to them, but also feel confident and comfortable in the relationship.

Select the right date and relationship

Before you put on your glad rags, book a table at a bistro and step out of the door, it's important to first find the right date. This is definitely a case of fools rush in, as dating anyone and everyone is a desperate measure and chances are it's doomed to failure.

If you have just come out of a relationship, my advice is to give yourself a break. Time allows you to grieve, heal wounds, release anger and get back to the old you. Taking any unfinished business into a new relationship really is a complete no-no.

Reflect on what it is you really want out of life and how a partner will fit into that. If you want to settle down and have kids pretty quickly, you need to make sure you go for the right person. Dating someone who is young and has ambitions to travel the world, work abroad and have lots of fun is not necessarily the one who's going to build a nest with you.

Consider their educational background and the kind of work you want a new partner to be doing, but don't restrict yourself. And remember, opposites do attract. If you are worried about age gaps, don't be. My own rule of thumb is that 15 years either way is absolutely manageable. Let's face it, age gaps work for many.

Ask yourself whether you think dating should be a means to an end. In other words, are you hoping to find a lasting relationship or are you dating for fun and to explore the possibilities? Both are absolutely fine, of course. Generally, most people choose to start dating as a journey of exploration and later move on to finding a partner. Be absolutely clear about whether you are exploring or wanting to settle down, as this can help you to make decisions about when to stay in a relationship and when to move on to the next one.

> ❝ Let's face it, age gaps
> work for many ❞

Accurate self-awareness is also important when dating or thinking about finding a new partner. For example, if you are a spontaneous person who enjoys spur-of-the-moment decisions, you may get bored and irritated in a relationship with someone who is more logical and insists on planning things out. And if you are an easygoing person, you may get frustrated with someone who is constantly uptight and a worrier. If you're not sure how you come across to others, ask one or two people who you trust and who will give you a fair assessment of yourself.

Being aware of how you want to be treated and how you expect to see a future partner behave will help you to know when someone is right for you or not. This will help you to go out with confidence and find the right person for you and you will be able to end dates and relationships quickly, without the emotional damage we can suffer. Above all, if you feel uncomfortable around someone you are dating, it just isn't going to work. In that case, end it.

Finding a date

This is, for many, the part that creates most frustration and wasted energy. If you have been off the dating circuit for some time, it can initially seem a bit scary, but things have changed and it might be a lot easier for you to find someone than you think.

The best way by far is to look for dates via people you already know, especially if you have an active social circle. The good thing about this is that you will already have an inside track on the potential date through your friends and will be able to make a judgement call as to whether they are right for you.

If you are desperate to go on some dates and haven't a clue where to start, think creatively about how you can expand your pool of potential dates. Think about joining social groups, taking up a new hobby or joining interest groups – all are great ways to meet new people.

Now, I know you may be thinking that the idea of placing a personal advertisement online is a bit naff, but it should be seriously considered. I have plenty of friends who met by joining an online dating service or placing a personal. For the executives out there who think that this might be a bit beneath them, try the broadsheets, as these newspapers now carry a section dedicated to love-hungry professionals.

Also, don't be shy to let all your friends know that you have the desire to meet someone new. Word of mouth is the best form of advertising, so go for it!

Be realistic

It can be really helpful to your confidence if you approach dating with a realistic attitude. Having realistic expectations about who will date you is important, as getting rejected and dumped regularly will sap your confidence faster than the particles spinning around the Hadron Collider.

Bear in mind that a date is like a bulb you plant in the garden. It will grow with the right conditions, without them it won't. The worst thing you can do is rush into a date and expect it to be instantly intimate. Human dynamics just don't work like that. Do I believe in love at first sight? Maybe. However, in the real world, this happens to the few rather than the many. So don't rush in expecting to agree plans for the wedding, the house and how many kids you think you should have. Take each date for what it is and enjoy it. And remember, the date may become a friend rather than a lover, and in many cases that's not a bad thing.

Do remember that the person you meet may be nice in their own right but just not for you. And if it's a blind date, remember there is no such thing as a horror story. We are all different, and this blind date could just be very different from you. Plan an exit strategy ahead of time, in case it does become painful, by arranging pre-planned phone calls to your mobile. You also need to remember that if someone does the same to you, it isn't about you and who you are. It just means that you are not for them. Keep it all in perspective and you will keep your confidence strong.

Only the minority of dates work out. Don't be surprised if you have 20 or even 30 dates before you find the one that lights your fire, so be patient. Don't let it get you down if things don't work out the first time – feel confident that you are on a learning curve that will find the right person for you. Stay positive and remember that we have all been there!

The first date

Think through carefully how you want to set up the first date. Before you go on the first date, make sure you play some mind games to boost your confidence and be completely sure you have let go of old relationships by practising some of the techniques in chapter 1 .

Some people like intimate dates over dinner and others like short and informal dates in a quiet pub. In short, do what suits you. If you feel comfortable, your confidence will be strong. My own opinion is that short and informal is best for the first date because if they aren't for you, you know it won't be long before you will be saying good-bye.

If you do like each other then, of course, if the feelings are mutual, make plans to spend more time with each other.

Always protect your safety by meeting in a public place with others around and, if you are a woman, let someone else know where you plan to go. Never meet someone at your home. This is not only risky, but if you have some jerk sitting on your sofa making him or herself comfortable for the night, it can get a bit awkward when you want to tell them to sod off!

Show your confidence

Practise the mind games from chapter 4 before you go on the date, to make sure your level of confidence is high. Practise some of my chill tips also, to help you relax, and be sure you have cleared out the garbage from the past. Get the internal and external branding razor-sharp – know what's going to make you interesting and dress so that you show your own style without going off the wall and scaring the natives.

A relaxed posture will help project confidence when you meet your date. As you engage in conversation, maintain steady eye contact and think positive thoughts about your date. It's amazing what they will pick up subliminally from you. As you chat, be friendly and warm and show confidence by expressing your opinions. If you disagree, don't panic, as this will add flavour to the conversation and will build respect for you.

Don't be afraid if you feel the other person isn't too keen on you. For all you know, you may be misreading them and if not, it's their loss. Keep holding up signs in your head which state that you are a worthwhile person in your own right, as this will help your confidence. As you sit there, mentally remind yourself that you are calm, comfortable and confident. The most important thing is to enjoy it and forget about what you 'should' or 'could' be doing. Be you!

Getting intimate

When you meet someone that floats your boat, what follows is a growing intimacy. As this develops, it can mean you become a little vulnerable because you become more open, but try to keep your confidence strong. Forget forcing intimacy, as this will simply have the opposite effect. Instead, let the process take its course and be patient!

I'm saying all this with respect to emotional intimacy; when it comes to sexual intimacy things are slightly different. Generally speaking, it doesn't take so long for natural arousal to increase and it's quite common for daters to have a sexual relationship early on. When it comes to sexual relations, be confident in your desires and enjoy the indulgence.

Commitment phobia

Commitment phobia is the fear of committing to anything and it is a common problem that can stop people from developing a long-term relationship. Commitment phobia can affect almost any part of the person's life, but it especially affects how a person feels about becoming involved, or staying involved, in a long-term relationship. It is often rooted in a deep fear of being emotionally hurt. A relationship commitment phobic will avoid ties and any obligations, but deep inside may really crave the stability that a long-term relationship can bring.

The problem for them is that they constantly run scared when it comes to dating and therefore sabotage any opportunity to begin a long-term relationship.

The commitment phobic will actually desire love and a long-term connection, but just can't seem to make it happen, often because of previous dysfunctional or abusive relationships, intimacy issues or childhood experiences.

Overcoming relationship commitment phobia is about letting go of the past (remember, the past is past) and giving yourself permission to trust again. Remember that commitment can be safe and that the majority of relationships are going to start off on solid foundations. If you feel you could do with support with commitment phobia, consider working with a well-respected confidence coach.

Walking away

Some of you may want to quit your current relationships but are not confident enough to take action, and this could be for a whole host of reasons. If you are suffering domestic abuse, please be assured that you are not alone and can get help. Women's Aid is a one of a number of networks that can offer advice and practical support – www.womensaid.org.uk.

It may be that you have lost the will and motivation to move on from a relationship that's lost its magic, and your confidence may have been worn down by a partner's negativity or you may simply be fearful of the change and being on your own again. Here's a checklist that could be useful to measure your current level of confidence in your relationship against your ability to move on if you feel you really need to.

	Yes	No
Do you think about being in a relationship with someone else?		
Do you mostly feel optimistic about your relationship?		
When you think about your current relationship does your heart tell you that you are not happy?		
Do you feel loved?		
Have you talked to your partner about improving your relationship?		
Could you tell your partner that it's over?		
Could you write down an exit strategy now?		

Dating: the script

The following script is designed to install positive suggestions into your mind, so that your confidence to date and develop a lasting relationship will increase. To use the script, simply sit comfortably in a quiet, warm room, place your hands on your thighs, relax deeply by letting all your muscles become heavy and tired and then count down slowly from ten to one. Once you are relaxed, slowly read the script to yourself. Alternatively you may get someone to read the script to you slowly, as you relax comfortably with your eyes closed. If you choose to do this, it is best to signal that you are ready to begin by simply lifting one of your index fingers rather than speaking out loud, so that your relaxation isn't disturbed. Notice that there are intervals between certain words to help ensure the script sinks deep into your mind.

As you relax ... comfortable and calm ... I want you to know that these things I say to you ... expressly stated for your benefit ... will begin ... slowly and surely to sink deeper and deeper into your unconscious mind ... so much so that your ability to date and form a lasting relationship ... will increase ... ever more deeply ... these suggestions will automatically enhance your ability ... to go on a date ... feel confident ... calm ... and at ease with yourself ...

And because you have let go of any negative past dating experiences ... you feel free ... free from anxiety about dating ... any unnecessary nervous tension melts away ... in fact you can smile to yourself ... giggle to yourself ... knowing that you ... can have fun and enjoy the dating game ... it is so comforting and relaxing ... to know that you are so at ease . . . melting into relaxation as we continue . . . feeling confident and more comfortable too . . .

I want you to know that . . . you will be at ease with yourself when dating . . . as soon as you know you have a date . . . you will feel calm . . . at ease with yourself . . . because you feel confident . . . confident in your own skin . . . confident about yourself . . . and because you feel confident about yourself . . . you will naturally be at ease with yourself . . . as you go on dates . . .

These things I say to you . . . affirm deeper and deeper into your mind . . . as you relax . . . comfortably and calmly . . . that as soon as you leave to go on a date . . . you will feel composed . . . confident, with your head held high . . . knowing that the dating game is fun . . . and that you are who you are . . . and that you like yourself for who you are . . . and it is . . . because you like yourself for who you are . . . that you will exude a natural warmth and confidence on that date . . .

As you arrive at the venue for the date . . . you walk tall . . . your posture relaxed . . . feeling open and comfortable as you walk towards your date . . . and as soon as you meet your date . . . you simply relax . . . feel at ease . . . feel so completely comfortable . . . because you know that you are comfortable and confident . . . you smile and greet your date with warm eye contact . . . in fact . . . you find the dating game fun . . . it's as if you are feeling that curious sense of excitement . . . ready to enjoy the relaxed company of your date . . .

As the date progresses you . . . allow yourself to remain

you ... feeling at ease as you ... share your own opinions about what it is you discuss ... you are happy to be you ... contented and at ease with being you ... because you feel so naturally confident on the date ... so confident in your own skin ... so comfortable and relaxed ... that the conversation flows easily and readily ... in fact ... you feel so completely comfortable that ... you project a confidence that affects your date ... who notices your open body language ... because you are so calm ... comfortable and confident too ...

You know that you have the choice ... to continue the date or to walk away ... because you are confident in yourself ... in your own being ... comfortable and secure in yourself ... in control and confident ... you also know that you can request to see your date again ... and ... because of your confidence ... you readily and easily request to see your date ... if you wish to see your date again ... calmly and comfortably ... respecting that your date also has the right to walk away ... because you know ... that dating is fun and it is a matter of pot luck ... and that if your date wishes to walk away they can ... because you understand that ... if your date walks away, you are still complete ... relaxed and comfortable ... you are unique and so are other people ... you feel calm and understand that ... people are different ... have different tastes ... so much so, you feel completely at ease with the dating game ... comfortable with dating ... and comfortable with you ...

Real Life

Susie

Susie was left on her own with two young children at the age of 39, after her partner died in a road traffic accident two years prior to her visiting me. She had lost all her natural confidence following the death of her partner and felt guilty about dating again, as she felt it betrayed his memory.

We spent a full session discussing the past and her guilt and, quite understandably, Susie was emotional as she said that she felt she was letting her former husband down. I worked delicately with Susie, helping her to let go of the past by getting her to communicate with her former partner in a hypnosis session. During session two, Susie said that she had moved forward and appreciated that her husband would understand and appreciate her moving on.

Susie hadn't dated for over 20 years and completely lacked confidence at the thought of dating someone who could turn out to be a new partner. I worked with her to help her to learn to relax and we then embarked on some mind games to help increase the self-belief and confidence that she sorely lacked.

Susie agreed that, to help stretch her confidence, she would make herself practise engaging in conversations with complete strangers. She highlighted the fact that she had a friend who she said could talk to anyone and would be a great role model to copycat. She watched her mate and talked to her about how and why she found it so easy to talk to other people.

Susie decided to join an online dating agency and before long was dating regularly. She wrote down a list of the qualities her Mr Right would have, so that she had a better chance of meeting someone who she knew she could get on with. She's still looking, but with a big smile on her face.

Martin

Martin was a 53-year-old introverted guy who'd spent his life working as a surveyor. He was very handsome, but he had very little outward confidence. He'd had one long-term relationship in his 30s, but had been dumped, and he'd not dated seriously since. He'd come to a point in his life when he wanted to find his perfect partner to spend the rest of his life with.

Martin readily admitted that he had zero confidence. Over six weeks, we worked through all the 7 Secrets of Confidence, to build him up to be supremely confident.

There were issues from the broken relationship in his 30s and a disrupted home life as a kid, so it was important to let these past issues go, as well as realising that he didn't have to be perfect to be accepted by a future partner.

The thought of going on a first date filled Martin with horror, so teaching him how to relax was critical before moving on to increasing his belief in himself and eliminating the fear of dating using the phobia fix mind game. Martin's image was pretty dated and he agreed to wardrobe-weed and buy a few new outfits to help boost his brand and make him feel more confident.

He agreed to stretch his confidence by attending a relaxed dating event at a local bar, which he actually loved. Finally, we implemented the copycat strategy by checking out how some of his friends always seemed to get the girls they wanted.

Martin also agreed that he would use the dating script to continue to build his confidence.

Nine months on, Martin got back in touch and told me that he had never had so much fun when dating, felt more at ease with himself, but wasn't quite ready to settle down. Martin had at last found his confidence and was going to make sure that any future long-term relationship was the right one.

Your secrets

- Know yourself – write down what's good about you and what would appeal to a potential date. If you can't do this objectively, ask one or two of your friends for their assessments.

- Think about the type of partner and date that you are looking for and think about what you want – is it fun with no strings or something longer-lasting and more meaningful?

- If you go on a blind date, don't have high expectations and be over-critical of who you meet.

- Practise the confidence-building mind games and make sure you have your mind-made armour on if you need it. Remember that dating can involve being rejected!

Confident in Social Situations

Too shy to shine

Shyness is a commonly felt emotion experienced by millions of people all over the world. Some are able to manage it, but in many cases it can be debilitating to the point where people are not being able to face any social situation. Of course, many of us feel nervous before meeting new people, but usually, once the conversation is flowing, we cope and even enjoy ourselves.

Extreme cases of shyness can result in the development of social phobia and even panic attacks. People who develop social phobia generally get very anxious about the prospect of meeting people and going into public situations. The confidence bucket in these cases is empty, and often these people worry that they will be criticised or something embarrassing will happen.

I know this only too well, as about 15 years ago I suffered from social phobia to the point where I quit my job and became fearful about speaking in front of other people. I avoided social situations, such as going to concerts, restaurants and the pub. I would really worry that other people were looking at me and judging me, and my ability to assert myself was dead. The confidence I'd had had run for the hills. Prior to this, I had been the life and soul of the party and now I couldn't even step through the door. Even at work and in business meetings I would make every excuse to escape, such as visiting the toilet every five minutes. My life had hit a real low.

> " Anxiety increases as you become worried about the anxiety "

If you have a social phobia, you may find yourself hovering around the door, not able to go into a room where other people are. And if you are able to walk through the door, you will probably feel everyone is looking at you. Some people may even feel worried about making a fool of themselves in front of others, or feel very anxious before going into social situations, and when they do, they may start stammering, trembling or feeling dizzy and faint. Of course, what then happens is that the symptoms make things even worse. Anxiety increases as you become worried about the anxiety. It can therefore become a self-fulfilling prophecy.

What eventually can happen is that the social anxiety intensifies and panic attacks set in. Panic attacks are damn awful things. In summary, they are severe attacks of anxiety and fear which come on suddenly, sometimes without warning. Symptoms are varied, but can include palpitations, fear of heart attack, dizziness, feeling faint, pins and needles and shortness of breath. My own experience tells me that an increase in self-confidence can significantly eliminate the social anxiety and panic attacks.

When I developed my own levels of confidence, my panic attacks stopped.

Accept first, then act

If you need to increase your confidence in social situations, first you need to accept that this is the way things are. Simply acknowledge that you are the way you are, but things can be done to help you move forward, and this is the first step. You are certainly not alone if you have a debilitating social phobia.

Next, I want you to reframe your anxiety and turn it into excitement. Begin from this moment forward to see anxiety as the same emotion as the excitement you feel when you are about to go on a fairground ride for the first time.

Learn to relax

With your central nervous system under fire and on fire from anxiety, it's critical that you learn to relax. Being in a constant state of anxiety in social situations is not good for you and can, over time, cause serious, damaging illness. You really need to convince your mind that things are okay and that you are safe and secure. The starting point for this is relaxation.

Practise some of the chill tips outlined in chapter 3 to start conditioning your mind and body to be more relaxed. Consider working with a clinical hypnotherapist, as they are professionally trained in how to help induce relaxation. It's also a good idea to take daily exercise, so that more endorphins are released, and combine this with a healthy diet. The endorphin rush is your body's natural high and it will help you to feel more confident.

Mind games are a must

It's important to play mind games when you are in a relaxed state to help increase your self-belief. Select the ones that suit you best. Command and deliver is a good technique to start with, as this will help to begin to affirm your self-confidence. Try the body armour mind game to help protect you from anxiety in social situations and practise dissociate and reintegrate to help programme your mind more constructively.

Stretch

Relaxation and mind games alone will not provide the solution and boost your confidence in social situations. It is really important to identify a few situations where you can put your toe in the water and stretch your confidence. Consider attending a few networking events, even if it is for half an hour. If you are invited to a party full of strangers, stretch your confidence by accepting the invite, even if you only attend for a short time. When you attend these social functions, stretch your confidence by engaging in small talk with people and start to notice how you feel natural and comfortable. The anxiety has melted away.

> Try the body armour mind game to help protect you from anxiety in social situations

Anxiety about anxiety: the script

People often tell me that their anxiety in social situations often comes from a fear of becoming anxious. The root of this may be that you have struggled on several occasions with hyper anxiety and limited confidence in a number of social situations, and you have reached a point where you automatically become anxious about getting anxious when you meet strangers. To get over this, I have developed a script designed to help alleviate anxiety about anxiety.

To use the script, sit comfortably in a quiet, warm room, place your hands on your thighs, relax deeply by letting all your muscles become heavy and tired and then count down slowly from ten to one. Once you are relaxed, slowly read the script to yourself. Alternatively, you may ask someone to read the script to you slowly, as you relax comfortably with your eyes closed. If you choose to do this it is best to signal that you are ready to begin by lifting one of your index fingers rather than speaking out loud, so that your relaxation isn't disturbed. Notice that there are intervals between certain words to help ensure the script sinks deep into your mind.

As you relax ... completely in control of yourself ... you are focusing on what you hear ... and can listen carefully ... to what I am telling you for your benefit ... to help you ... to reduce your anxiety ... and you will remember everything that I am going to tell you ... and because of these things that I tell you ... you will feel very good ... very good about yourself ... and the world around you ... you will use what you hear for your benefit ... you will remember what I tell you and use it every day ... whenever you feel anxious ... you will remember what I tell you ... as you relax ... you will concentrate on what I tell you very well . . . and do what I tell you . . . for your benefit . . .

And I want you to know that . . . whenever you become anxious . . . you will realise that the reason you are becoming anxious . . . is that you are being hard on yourself . . . telling yourself that you must do this . . . or you must do that . . . or you must be this . . . or you must be that . . . you will be aware that anxiety is triggered . . . by what you say to yourself . . . it doesn't come from other people . . . it comes from what you say to yourself . . . and you will be very aware of this . . . you become anxious because of the demands you put on yourself . . . you will be very aware of this . . . knowing this is really good . . . because you know that you can control this . . .

You will realise that you have the control over anxiety . . . you will realise that you don't have to keep making yourself anxious or over-excited . . . if you give up telling yourself what you must or should do . . . you will say to yourself . . . if I accept what is . . . accept the way things are, then I won't be overly anxious . . . you will remind yourself by saying to yourself . . . I can make myself less anxious and less tense by giving up the musts . . . the shoulds . . . simply by relaxing about the way things are . . . and knowing that I am okay with the way things are . . .

And you will keep telling yourself . . . I am okay . . . I feel okay about myself . . . I am at ease with myself . . . and my over-excitement won't kill me . . . there are lots of unpleasant things that I don't like . . . but I can put up with them . . . I cope with them . . . I don't have to avoid them or get rid of them . . . you will tell yourself that

if you're over-excited, then you are over-excited...
and you will be sure in the knowledge that...you
can learn from these feelings...even if they are
uncomfortable...remembering that you can say to
yourself that you don't have to do anything you don't
want to do and...that you don't have to succeed...
you will remember that what makes us unhealthy is
the idea that...we have to be like this...or that...
or we have to get rid of the anxiety or over-
excitement...

Each day you will hear this script...and you will put
what you learn into practice...and when you feel anxious
or over-excited...you will look at what you are
doing...to make yourself anxious...and you will let go
of the demands you put on yourself...you will smile as
you challenge the idea that you have to be like this...or
have to be like that...in fact, you will ask yourself...why
do I have to do so well?...I don't...you will realise
that you don't need approval...you may like it...but
you realise you don't need it...you will even smile as you
remind yourself by saying to yourself...I'd like to be
like this, but I don't need to be like it...knowing that
none of these things you fail at are going to kill you...

As you begin to tell yourself...that even if you get so
over-excited or anxious that you lose control...that's
okay...you will remember that if you tell yourself...I
must not lose control...you will lose control...but, of
course, even if you do lose control, you can live with
it...you can stand it...you will remember that nothing
is the end of the world...nothing is that bad...and
you can tolerate what is uncomfortable because...you
are strong...stronger than you think...you even think

that if people don't like you, that's okay ... even if you act absurdly, even when you are anxious, that is okay ...

You are going to think these things every day ... whenever you become over-excited or anxious ... you will see clearly what you are over-excited or anxious about ... you will realise you are demanding something of yourself ... saying you must be like this ... or you must be like that ... you must calm down or you must not make a mistake ... and when you hear yourself saying these things, you will see a bright-red stop sign ... and in your mind shout the word 'NO' loudly ... this is crap ... and say to yourself that if these things happen to me then they happen to me ... it isn't the end of the world ... I'd like not to be anxious ... I'd like to be friends with everyone ... but if I'm not, then it's not the end of the world ... I can still be happy ...

You will continue to keep using your logical mind to remind yourself ... remind yourself of all these things I tell you ... to focus on letting go of the over-excitement ... just as you are concentrating right now ... and your ability to use your thinking in this way ... will get better and better ... you are going to be more in control of your thoughts and feelings ... you will realise more and more that ... you create your feelings of over-excitement ... you make yourself anxious and you don't have to ... you can give up your over-excitement ... by giving up your demands ... and you can relax ... relax ... relax ... relax ... relax ...

And this is what you are going to remember ... and continue to work at ... you will take the idea that you are in control...saying to yourself daily...I control me...there is no need to upset myself...about anything...of course...with all my new learning...I realise that if I do upset myself...it wouldn't be nice...but it's not the end of the world...and it's not that terrible...I may be upset for a while, but it will pass...and you will now realise that...you can easily say to yourself...I can be over-anxious...or excited...without putting myself down...without saying I must not be anxious...

You are going to get so efficient and effective...better and better...about thinking in this way...you will be more in control of you...of course never totally in control because no one is ever totally in control...and that is, of course, okay...but you will be less anxious and less over-excited...because of the way you now think...knowing that nothing is that bad...nothing is that terrible...not even uncomfortable feelings...that is what you are going to continue to realise and keep thinking until you really believe it...

You will now begin to release yourself from over-excitement or anxiety...all by yourself...you can... right now...accept yourself...accept your feelings... and stop telling yourself...from this moment forward ...I must not be anxious...instead, tell yourself...these feelings are unwanted...and I will now work on them to change them...I will from now on challenge my demands...I am in control...

Real Life

Josh

Josh, a 43-year-old self-employed builder, married with twins, came under massive personal pressure as the construction industry declined during the recession. He began to feel the pressure as clients dropped contracts and mothballed plans. He began to self-doubt, blame himself for not being a good enough builder and his confidence went down like a ton of bricks.

He had an impressive track record, but had never experienced such a severe downturn and became lost in trying to keep track of mortgage payments and bills.

Over a period of four weeks, Josh went from an extroverted personality to one that was distant, socially fragile and introspective. He'd been used to working with small groups of other guys on projects, but now he couldn't face them, as his business tumbled down around him.

Josh was recommended to visit me by one of his colleagues, whom I had previously supported. As soon as I met Josh, I could appreciate that his self-confidence had plummeted and his stress levels were through the roof. He told me that he was suffering from a sudden lack of confidence in social and work settings and needed immediate support. He was also feeling a state of prolonged anxiety and reported feeling dizzy in the company of others.

I worked with Josh over four sessions, initially training him in how to relax and utilise the dissociation and reintegration technique. We also went through a one-to-one hypnotherapy session and incorporated the command and deliver mind game.

Session two involved a further spell of hypnotherapy, utilising the confidence room, followed by the soap opera mind game. In addition, I conducted confidence training to ensure Josh understood and felt that his confidence was returning and that he was in control. I also set homework at the second session, which was for Josh to read the anxiety about anxiety script twice a day.

At session three, Josh was making good progress. He reported his anxiety had reduced and that he was more at ease around work colleagues. His thought processes had changed and he was less anxious about being anxious. During session three, I again delivered a hypnotherapy session which was designed to seal Josh's confidence. To do this, I used the stroke the ego mind game, ensuring his unconscious mind was programmed and more confident.

Josh worked through the difficult times of the credit crunch and managed to just keep his business ticking over. Josh is a good example of what a difference it makes to catch anxiety problems early before they take all confidence away and leave the person at rock bottom. Do something before the shit hits the fan.

Linda

At 44, finance director Linda came to see me, explaining that she was starting to suffer from panic attacks. Linda had visited her GP and been prescribed anti-depressants, so it was important that I worked closely with her GP.

Together, Linda and I planned a structured programme of six sessions to alleviate the panic attacks and increase her confidence, a plan I often use to help clients who suffer from panic attacks.

Session 1: A detailed case history was taken from Linda, so that I fully understood the history of the condition and could set a goal for the process. Linda explained that her goal was to alleviate panic and increase self-confidence.

Session 2: I delivered a full hypnotherapy session, which included the command and deliver mind game and the anxiety about anxiety script. Linda was also given homework to read the script twice daily.

Session 3: I used something known as symptom scaling. I helped Linda relax and, with her eyes closed, she explored the feelings of fear and started to appreciate that fear is a similar emotion to anxiety. With Linda hypnotised, I asked her to bring in a contrasting emotion, in this case relaxation. Linda was then asked to scale how she felt between one and ten, with one being completely relaxed. This process proved to Linda that she was in control and she could experience both fear and relaxation. While she was still hypnotised, I got her to take the relaxation into the future. Linda enjoyed this session immensely, as it proved that she could experience a relaxed state if she put her mind to it.

Session 4: I conducted a full session of stroke the ego, programming Linda's mind that she was in control, relaxed, more at ease and that she was able to be who she wanted to be. Linda was also once again asked to read the anxiety about anxiety script. I then utilised what's called a paradoxical intervention by asking Linda to deliberately have a panic attack. Of course, she couldn't effectively bring up a panic attack because the more we try to do something, the harder it is. Linda welcomed this principle, recognising that the more she tried to fight panic and anxiety, the more likely it was going to be triggered, but if she could relax, it was far less likely to occur.

Session 5: I worked on one of Linda's specific goals. Linda had made excellent progress and was feeling much more in control. She explained that she was to have a new boss, in this case a new chief executive. Focusing on this area where confidence was required, I delivered a clinical hypnotherapy session and used the soap opera and fine fusion mind games. Linda went away feeling positive and more in control and, I observed, more naturally confident. She was able to confidently meet her new CEO, look her in the eye and communicate effectively. Back of the net!

Session 6: At the final session, Linda and I conducted a full session of clinical hypnotherapy, utilising progressive relaxation and several mind games. I finished off with the confidence room mind game, explaining to Linda outside of the hypnotherapy session how she could use the copycat strategy.

Linda got in touch later to tell me that she was now free from the anti-depressants and back to being who she once was. I asked her what the turning point had been and she replied, 'Appreciating what anxiety about anxiety is and how it hung around my neck like a bloody great chain. Following on from this realisation, I can affirm all the time that I believe in myself.'

Your secrets

- You're not alone – social phobia is very common and you should understand that all sorts of people have experienced a social phobia.

- Relax, there's nothing to be scared of – get the relaxation techniques under your belt and you'll replace anxiety with relaxation, feeling and appearing confident.

- Stretch yourself – give yourself a programme where you plan and execute being in social situations that start to stretch you.

- If you suffer from panic attacks, consider contacting a professionally qualified clinical hypnotherapist for support. Visit www.stevemiller training.com for more information.

Confident Conversationalist 12

I t isn't unusual on my business travels to meet many executives who, when they stand up and deliver a presentation to 500 people, are engaging and inspiring. But when it comes to holding a one-to-one conversation, I often find them feeling a little awkward, tongue-tied, and flustered.

Many people struggle and become tongue-tied if they have to get involved in one-to-one expressive conversations, especially with people they don't know. This is a fact borne out in our survey, so in this chapter I will put some key tools into your hands to help you feel more confident and self-assured. I'll have you talking one-to-one with more confidence than Jonathan Ross.

I have learnt over the years that there are three important ground rules when it comes to holding a good conversation. The first is that it is better to be interested in others than act like Narcissus's reflection and bang on about yourself. The second is that if you can show that you are willing to give someone else your undivided attention, it is highly flattering. Finally, it is best to let people talk about themselves. Conversation cannot be all about you; it has to be about the other person as well. That way you can make your conversation more engaging and natural.

> " I'll have you talking one-to-one
> with more confidence than
> Jonathan Ross "

All about them

Remember to place emphasis on them, not you, and be sure to take responsibility for kick-starting the conversation. If you are among strangers, there is nothing wrong with introducing yourself confidently. Stretch your confidence by approaching a stranger and simply saying, 'Hi, I thought I'd say hello and introduce myself.' Thereafter, the conversation begins to flow.

As much as you might enjoy being centre stage, allow the other person to have their time in the limelight. In other words, stroke them and they will adore you. As you speak with the person, be sure to maintain eye contact and nod occasionally, so that you endorse what is being said, unless, of course, you disagree, in which case you should either stay neutral or express your disagreement assertively.

A great way to encourage someone to talk is by asking them open-ended questions. These questions will start with how, what, why, where and when. People love to feel they can talk about themselves and by asking open-ended questions, you really will make them feel special. Naturally, when someone answers your question, make sure you listen actively to their response, otherwise it will just seem as though you are asking questions for the sake of asking questions, implying that you are fake. When you are in this listening mode, it becomes much easier to ask follow-up questions and the conversation will confidently roll on.

Rapport during a conversation can be made stronger by using the person's name, as this shows you are interested in them. As the conversation moves forward and the other person answers your questions, put them at ease by smiling and offering nods, which help affirm that you are listening and continues to build strong rapport. When you talk, do your best to link what you say to the other person's interests.

Encouraging phrases

The following phrases will help you to confidently engage with other people effectively, as they encourage the flow of conversation:

- That sounds really interesting, tell me more about it

- Can you give me some examples of that?

- What would you like to see happen in the future?

- How do you feel about that now?

- Where do you think this will all lead to?

- Why do you think they decided to do it that way?

Bodies speak volumes

As you engage in conversation, it really is important that you demonstrate body language that is open (i.e. don't stand there with your arms folded), encouraging and, of course, confident. You don't want to become a submissive number two in the conversation; you want to remain an equal who is warm and inviting. Getting your body language right will help the flow of the conversation and portray you as interested, interesting and confident. Follow my tips for effective body language and you will not only look confident, but sound and feel like you are as well.

1   Take up space and be visible. Confident people like to take up some space. In other words, don't sit in a chair in a corner with your legs crossed or shy away into the distance in a room full of people. When speaking to someone, avoid hiding behind your hair or covering your mouth with your hand, as this will block the natural flow of the conversation.

2   Make inviting eye contact and maintain it. Confident people look others in the eye. Do be aware, however, that this may differ in certain cultures. Avoid a hard gaze, but offer warm eye contact and practise smiling with your eyes. Remember to think good thoughts about the person you are looking at, as these feelings will transmit unconsciously to the other person.

3   Keep your chest up. Confident people will keep their chests broad and upright, rather than dropped. Of course, I am not suggesting you walk around sticking your chest

out. The rule is to keep it upright and flexible, rather than hunched and jelly-like. This will also help you to speak clearly and with confidence.

4 Head held high. As a confident person you will hold your head upright, as opposed to looking at the floor, as you engage in conversation with the other person. This, along with good eye contact, will project your confidence to the other person.

5 Face says it all. Confident people let their faces say the right things at the right time. It's no good smiling and laughing if the conversation is about something serious. Remember, your body and words should say the same thing.

6 Relaxed body and sharp mind. Confident people maintain a relaxed body language. They breathe freely, easily and deeply, instead of laboured, shallow, fast or irregular breathing.

7 Gesture but not overload. Confident people do use their hands to express themselves. To do this, make sure your fingers are in a spread position rather than tangled. Use gentle rather than busy gestures to express what you are saying to the other person. Busy gestures will just confuse the conversation, whereas gentle gesturing will help express what it is you are saying.

8   Perfect posture. It may sound an old cliché but remember to stand up straight. It really is one of the most important body language behaviours associated with confidence. Show your full height and you will appear confident in the conversation. This doesn't mean you are trying to intimidate the other person; you are simply expressing your confidence in a way which isn't aggressive.

Chill and play your mind games

If you do find it difficult to express yourself in one-to-one conversations, do practise relaxation, so that you learn to chill and not worry so much about yourself. Anxiety blocks expressive body language, so condition yourself to be more relaxed by practising some of the techniques in chapter 3. Consider also playing some of the mind games set out in chapter 4, as this will help set you up positively. Select the ones that suit you best and practise them for at least three weeks. It won't be long before you notice how at ease and more confident you feel.

Managing disagreement assertively

It is unlikely that you will have a straightforward, engaging conversation where you agree with the other person all of the time. There will be occasions when you will want to express your disagreement. Of course, as a confident individual, you will want to communicate assertively as opposed to submissively or aggressively. Being assertive means that you say what you want or feel while respecting the needs of the person you are in conversation with. It is being able to communicate constructively in a direct, open and honest way.

When in conversation with others, if we allow the other person's needs, opinions or judgements to become more important than our own, we may end up feeling hurt, angry and frustrated. It is therefore important to express yourself so that you maintain your self-respect and leave the conversation on a win-win basis. That is unless, of course, you confidently decide that to disagree assertively is not the right strategy to take, which is your right. Assertiveness is sometimes seen as the mid-point between passive and aggressive ways of projecting your character. There are a number of practical tips you can use to help build your assertive style:

1   Dress assertively. Make sure that you brand yourself like an exclusive product, so you look as though you respect yourself. If you look like junk, you will be treated like junk. We all know where junk generally ends up – discarded and in the bin.

2   Keep the body confident. Maintain the positive body language described earlier. Fifty-five per cent of communication is through the visual gestures of body language, so take on the tips above.

3   Keep calm and listen. Assertive people always listen first and then speak. As you listen, breathe deeply, relax and respect that the other person has the right to their opinion, even if you are thinking, 'Jerk'.

4   Use a calm, clear voice. Remember that you don't have to be loud, but you do need to make yourself heard. Use a calm voice that is well-paced, allowing each word to finish before you start the next.

5 Show empathy. Make sure you demonstrate empathy before you rush in with your own point of view. This will help the conversation be less confrontational and stressful. You can show empathy by simply reflecting back what the other person has said, such as, 'I can appreciate you are saying that the government have done ABC.' Other empathic statements are: 'I understand you are saying ABC' or 'I can see that you believe ABC.'

6 Know what you want to say. Once you have demonstrated empathy, you can then state what it is you want to say. For example: 'I appreciate you believe the government are right to do ABC, however, I would prefer they did DEF, as this would in my opinion get a result faster.' If you are interrupted, simply say, 'Allow me to finish and I will then listen to you.'

7 Broken record. If, when you have finished, the other person still disagrees, use what is known as the broken record technique. This is simply stating again what your point of view is, having again listened to the other person. If you continue to disagree, simply acknowledge that you will have to agree to disagree, and that's okay. Then calmly move on to another subject.

Be a confident conversationalist: the script

The following script is designed to embed positive suggestions into your mind, so that you become an expressive and engaging conversationalist. To use the script, simply sit comfortably in a quiet, warm room, place your hands on your thighs, relax deeply by letting all your muscles become heavy and tired and then count down slowly from ten to one. Once you are relaxed, slowly read the script to yourself. Alternatively, you can ask someone to read the script to you slowly, as you relax comfortably with your eyes closed. If you choose to do this, it is best to signal that you are ready to begin by lifting one of your index fingers rather than speaking out loud, so that your relaxation isn't disturbed. Notice that there are intervals between certain words to help ensure the script sinks deep into your mind.

As you sit relaxed, listening to these words . . . you may notice which part of you feels most relaxed . . . and . . . as you breathe freely and easily you can . . . in your own time . . . relax even more deeply . . . as you let go . . . let go of the unnecessary nervous tension . . . it can melt . . . melt completely . . . as you sink deeper and deeper into a warm, relaxed state . . . a state that will become more and more comfortable . . . as you become more and more at ease with yourself . . .

And I am going to speak with you . . . speak with you about a matter of importance to you . . . and I want you to know that . . . these things I say to you . . . all for your benefit . . . will sink deep into your mind . . . will be remembered . . . recalled . . . both inside and outside of this room . . . what I say will sink deep into your mind so that you become . . . automatically . . . more at ease with yourself . . . more confident about yourself as you engage in conversation with other people . . .

It is because you will be at ease with yourself that . . . you will notice how easy and relaxed you feel . . . both inside and outside of this room . . . to communicate one-to-one with other people . . . feeling relaxed . . . so that your conversation with other people is comfortable . . . at ease . . . and because you feel at ease with yourself . . . you are able to demonstrate positive and confident body language . . . you will stand tall as you engage in conversation with other people . . . your head held high . . . your infectious smile engaging others around you . . .

And as you stand comfortable . . . tall . . . head held high . . . your eye contact with the other person is gentle and comfortable . . . because you feel confident . . . you will feel so comfortable and confident as you engage in conversation with other people . . . it is because you feel at ease . . . you know that you are who you are and that is fine . . . and because you are happy with who you are . . . you are able to have open body posture . . . chest held upright . . .

And now you are so comfortable with being you . . . you are able and feel confident to introduce yourself to complete strangers . . . simply introducing yourself by name . . . and striking up a natural conversation or simply moving on . . . you notice how you are taking an interest in the other person . . . you listen carefully . . . and because you are relaxed about yourself . . . you are able to listen actively to what they are telling you . . . you take a natural and calm interest in other people . . .

As the conversation progresses, you are able to offer your free-flowing opinions . . . and . . . you will notice that you ask the other person questions . . . open-ended questions . . . questions that will automatically encourage the other person to continue speaking freely with you . . . as you ask these questions, you will also notice how good it feels to be interested in other people . . . and that they develop strong rapport with you . . . as you ask open-ended questions . . .

During the conversation, you will use open gestures . . . gestures that represent what you are saying . . . your gentle gestures make you more interesting and you feel confident . . . confident about yourself as you use gentle gestures that make you more interesting . . . because you are interesting . . . you now feel how interesting you are . . . and you will continue to acknowledge how interesting you are . . . because you are at ease with yourself . . . who you are . . . and what you stand for . . .

And you know that if you disagree when engaged in conversation with other people, you simply . . . relax and listen to the other person . . . you accept and agree that it is fine to disagree . . . that disagreement in conversation is healthy . . . it stimulates the engagement of the conversation . . . and it is okay . . . of course, it isn't an attack on you . . . it is part of you being interesting . . . and . . . when people disagree you will . . . listen . . . show empathy before stating your point of view . . . before expressing your own point of view . . . and if disagreement continues, you recognise it is okay to agree to disagree . . . you simply move on . . .

It is because you are now feeling relaxed...at ease...more comfortable with yourself...who you are...and at ease in conversation with people...that you are able to engage...and express yourself comfortably...both inside and outside of this room...and these things I say to you...now embed deeper and deeper into your mind...all for your benefit...that you will now engage in conversation with other people more naturally...more relaxed...because you are now becoming more confident...more confident about yourself...more confident about your abilities...talents...more confident about yourself...

Real Life

Richard

Richard was a 24-year-old graduate who'd landed his first job as a games developer, a job where he could keep his head down and do his own thing most of the time. He came to see me explaining that he didn't have the confidence to engage with people on a one-to-one basis, even if he knew them. He told me that he was continually uptight and had the feeling that he was always going to put his foot in his mouth if he started to talk to someone.

This was becoming more of a worry for Richard because he knew he had to become more able to engage in conversation with others if his career was going to take off, as he had to travel overseas to technology fairs and so on.

I went through two sessions with Richard. At the first session, I agreed with him that we would practise introductory one-to-one conversation, so that he could understand the fundamentals of engaging with someone else. After a shaky start, Richard began to enjoy the practice and soon became more confident and was looking forward to striking up conversations and asking open-ended questions.

At this first session, I also taught Richard how to induce relaxation, so that he could practise the soap opera mind game. In addition, we agreed on a number of tasks for Richard to stretch his confidence, including deliberately going out of his way to introduce himself and ask a couple of open-ended questions to work colleagues.

Between sessions, Richard didn't do very well. He struggled with the soap opera mind game in relaxation and made some weak attempts to stretch his confidence. He was downhearted and demotivated.

During session two, I confidence-coached Richard particularly to ask open questions to encourage and stimulate conversation and also to manage any disagreements that might come out of the growing number of conversations he was going to have. Struggling at first, he eventually understood and learnt how to communicate assertively. We put the icing on the cake by going through a session of clinical hypnotherapy and using the phobia fix, which Richard later told me had freed him up from the burden of being scared to talk to other people. Richard also agreed to go away and read the script twice daily.

In the coming months, Richard was able to work on the tools for conversation and shape himself into a confident and much more outgoing individual. He got himself in line for promotion and even felt the impact in his personal life, meeting someone at the big gaming show in Las Vegas — no Elvis chapel wedding please!

Ingrid

An academic at one of the UK's leading universities, 48-year-old Ingrid had a dazzling intellect that most of us can only admire from a distance. Yes, she was a genius but, on the other hand, she was, in her words, a total nerd who was a confidence bankrupt when it came to socialising and talking to others.

In a strange kind of way, I grew quite fond of Ingrid. She was eccentric, very individual and, again in her words, a typical spinster. I found her interesting and it was a great challenge to turn her into a social butterfly. That's exactly what she wanted to be and it chewed her up inside to think that she didn't have the confidence to approach interesting people and to think that they pre-judged her and dismissed her as a stereotyped 'professor'.

Ingrid was an analytical character and wanted to spend time understanding why she had this particular problem, delving into her past to pick out the skeletons that bound her social confidence. I told Ingrid straight-forwardly that, working with me, we would only spend a maximum of one hour assessing the past. We weren't going to pick over the bones of the past to find the possible cause of why she was like she was. If that's what she wanted, she would have to engage an analytical therapist, and you know what my opinion is on that lot. She smiled and said, 'Steve, I've tried that, got stuck to the couch and felt worse than I did when the therapy started'. We both laughed and agreed to move forward to get a rapid improvement in Ingrid's social confidence.

During the first session, we did spend the promised 60 minutes reviewing the past and drew closure on it, with Ingrid agreeing wholeheartedly that 'the past is past'. She went away feeling positive that she could now start to move forward, build her social confidence and reduce her anxiety about one-to-one conversations.

During sessions two and three, I focused on helping Ingrid become more relaxed about herself and I delivered two hypnotherapy sessions, using the mind game techniques that she preferred. At the final session, I conducted a one-to-one confidence-boosting session which included role play and a final practice. Ingrid was amazing! She held herself well, had a smile to die for and asked some great questions to help the conversations flow. I even got a friend of mine, a complete stranger to her, to come into a stretch session to see how she would cope. They got on like a house on fire and Ingrid was able to show me that she listened intently to what the other person was saying, asking open questions and sticking to the subject without going off on wild tangents.

Ingrid maintains close contact with me, updating me on her progress, and we have become good friends. She has developed into a little gem of a conversationalist.

Daisy

At 18, Daisy was referred to me by her mum, who was worried that her daughter, who was set to take up a place at one of the country's top universities to study law, would not have the confidence skills to get on with her peers and shine as a student.

I normally would have disagreed with her mum's opinion and suggested that university was the best place for Daisy to find herself, but Daisy called me herself and, in a very shy and mouse-like voice, pleaded with me to see her. This I did, as I thought she sounded like she was in desperate need of a confidence boost.

When we met, I could tell by her body language that she was unbelievably shy and that to really shine during her degree course, she needed to be able to come out of her shell. I explained that she could really boost her confidence if she started to look at the way she came across to other people, from her eye contact and her body language to the way she spoke. I asked her to come back into my consulting room as though she had not met me before — introducing herself in a confident voice and giving me a decent handshake, while making solid eye contact with me and holding my attention. The basics would show Daisy that some simple techniques could give a rapid shot of self-confidence if they were practised and executed correctly.

The other area that really concerned her was that she wanted to be able to make new friends that would be long-lasting and special to her. Being a naturally shy girl, she'd struggled to get to know many of her fellow students properly and admitted that she enjoyed the company of books more than that of girlfriends or boyfriends. What I did, which I knew would please Daisy, was to give her some homework to come up with natural introductions to conversations that she could use with fellow freshers. We also worked on other conversation skills, especially how to listen to others and show natural interest in and respect for what they are saying. We even moved on to how to deal with those who might be rude and overbearing and not show the same respect.

The transformation in Daisy's confidence was wonderful to see. In just a couple of months, she'd gone from the mouse who shuffled in to see me to a proud young woman with her head held high and the skills to engage and enthrall anyone she met. I got a lovely postcard from her thanking me for my help and telling me that she was sharing a big house with four other girls, was dating a guy regularly and was loving her course. It was a joy to hear that Daisy was blossoming.

7 Secrets of Confidence

- Put others before yourself when starting up new conversations.

- If you get feelings and sensations of anxiety just at the prospect of speaking to someone new, follow the chill tips in chapter 3.

- Conversation is about balancing being passive and assertive when it's appropriate – it's like great comedy, it's all about the timing.

- If things get sticky and someone is saying something you don't like, be assertive and tell them, but keep it calm and clear.

- Keep your body language open for communication – making eye contact and keeping your arms relaxed and not folded.

- Think of one or two open questions that will allow you to show interest in the person you are talking to and keep the conversation flowing.

Confident in Exams

13

Although it is not my own measure of a person's success or capabilities, we live in a society that increasingly promotes the academic route, prioritising passing exams and climbing the ladder through the gathering of professional qualifications. Indeed, our YouGov survey revealed that confidence to do well in exams is high on the agenda for the British public.

We know that qualifications are becoming more and more important to employers and it comes as no surprise that people want to empower their confidence to not only sit the examinations, but to have the self-belief that they will score well and have a bankable qualification at the end of the process.

> **Confidence to do well in exams is high on the agenda for the British public**

7 Secrets of Confidence

In this chapter, I will focus on boosting confidence, so that you are well positioned to sit and pass whatever exam it is you will be taking, be it your finals at university, your driving test or a vocational assessment. I also want to concentrate on improving your memory, one of those little advantages that can make the difference between a pass or a fail in an exam.

What is memory?

As many exams will test you on how to apply knowledge and facts, it's vital that you can recall them when they are needed. This can be a huge hurdle for people who become anxious about not being able to remember things they have read or points from papers they have produced in the past. You need to understand what your memory is and how it can become your biggest ally during exams.

There are many definitions of what our memory is. In short, it is the ability to retain information and recall information about previous experiences and things we have learnt. When we try to recall an experience or specific fact, a process takes place in which our brain will recover what it is we experienced or learnt. Just imagine the biggest library you can and someone has to dash around the shelves to pick out the right volume that contains the stored experience or relevant facts that you want. Some are near the front and easy to access, but others are buried high up and way back in the memory library.

There are two types of memory: short-term and long-term. Short-term memory is the recollection of your most recent knowledge and experiences. This is also known as the working memory. In other words, the information is what we are currently thinking about. This is also defined as the conscious mind. Most of the information in the working memory will be stored for around 30 seconds.

Long-term memory is the recollection of events and things

we've learnt from the past, going back days or years. The long-term memory is created in a series of processes. This is how it works: you have an experience and the brain registers it; it encodes it and, with the right conditions, will store it for later use. Long-term memory would be called the unconscious mind in Freudian psychology. Much of the long-term memory is outside our awareness, but in the right conditions can be confidently called into the working memory to be used as needed.

How to improve your memory

There is a range of mind games that I will go into that can be used to recall information from the long-term memory. However, let's begin with some top tips to help improve your memory.

1   Stop, look and listen. It really is important to pay attention to something you are trying to learn. You don't remember things you haven't fully learnt, so your focused concentration is critical. Focused concentration, in a quiet environment without interruption, will ensure you encode the learning and experience into your mind so that it can be recalled later.

2   Learn how you learn best. People tend to learn in a very visual manner, by reading or observing something being done. However, it may be that you are more of an auditory learner, in which case you will learn by listening. If this is you, consider recording lectures or buying CDs and listening to the information until you remember it.

3   Use all your senses. Do use as many senses as possible, so that your memory improves. For example, if you are an auditory learner, also read the information. If you are revising for exams, don't just read through the material, but write it out and then write it out again. Where appropriate, bring in other senses, such as smell and taste.

4   Link it all in. Link the new information to existing information you already remember. This can be new material that builds on your previous knowledge, such as knowing someone's telephone number and then learning what part of town they live in.

5   Organise the information. Try writing things down in notebooks, calendars and diaries and use words, pictures and colours to help organise the information into a meaningful and logical order.

6   Play the information over and over. When you learn something, go over it again and again the same day and regularly after that. The more you do this, the easier it will be to recall the information. Practise recalling the information over and over again and you will feel confident in your ability to recall it.

7   It's all about attitude. Motivation and positive attitude is king. If you want to learn something and you feel energised and motivated, it will be easier. And forget telling yourself you have a bad memory, as this will only make things difficult by automatically undermining your self-confidence. Think positively about your memory and your memory will work much better for you.

8   Use pictures. If you are a visual person, you may find it useful to use pictures. For example, a picture of a rose to remember the name Rosemary, or even a colour scheme to help you remember certain facts. If it works for you, use it!

9   Rhymes. Rhymes can help you to remember facts. For example: 'Thirty days hath September, April, June and November.' Try making up one of your own for certain pieces of information that you will need to recall in the exam.

10 Humour. Humour and jokes can help improve recall from your memory library. If you can create humour around what you want to remember, this is a great way to recall information because funny and odd things always stand out and are easier to remember.

Deep into the mind

When you revise for exams, it is helpful to use the following technique to transfer the information from short-term to long-term memory:

1   Identify three key facts you want to place deep into your mind.

2 Read them and write them down three times.

3 Induce a state of relaxation.

4 In relaxation, focus on the three facts and mentally say them to yourself three times.

5 Imagine those facts now drifting deep into your unconscious mind.

6 When you have finished, open your eyes and take a five-minute break before going on to learn the next three facts.

Relaxation and memory recall

One of the most powerful ways to recall from memory is to relax and mentally focus on requesting the unconscious mind to bring forward the information you seek. The reason this will work well for you is because when you relax, your conscious mind will rest and step to the side, so that your unconscious mind will release the information to you at the conscious level. By relaxing, the door between the conscious and unconscious mind slides open and the information is recalled. If you find yourself in an exam struggling to recall some important information, the harder you think of it the more difficult it will be to retrieve it. By simply taking a minute to close your eyes and relax, strange as it may seem, and then asking your unconscious mind to bring forward the information, you will be pleasantly surprised how the information gradually comes to you.

Set yourself up

As well as improving your memory, you can also set yourself up for exam success by playing a number of mind games to build your confidence. These could include:

1   Command and deliver – useful to self-affirm that you will be calm, relaxed and focused when you take the exam.

2   The confidence room – to help turn up your confidence for the exam itself.

3   Fine fusion – borrowing confident resources from a previous examination and mentally fusing them into the forthcoming exam.

4   Soap opera – seeing, hearing and feeling yourself performing confidently in the exam.

5   Phobia fix – to reframe your perception of the exam and feel comfortable and relaxed on the day of the exam.

6   Clear goal model – to help get into the zone and programme your behaviour for success in the exam.

Exam success: the script

This script is designed to embed positive suggestions into your mind for exam success. To use the script, sit comfortably in a quiet, warm room, place your hands on your thighs, relax deeply by letting all your muscles become heavy and tired and then count down slowly from ten to one. Once you are relaxed, slowly read the script to yourself. Alternatively, you can ask someone to read the script to you slowly, as you relax comfortably with your eyes closed. If you choose to do this, it is best to signal that you are ready to begin by lifting one of your index fingers rather than speaking out loud, so that your relaxation isn't disturbed. Notice that there are intervals between certain words to help ensure the script sinks deep into your mind.

As you relax . . . I want you to notice . . . that when you do relax . . . you think more clearly . . . calmly . . . and because you are now relaxed . . . you are calm . . . your free-flowing thoughts can flow even more freely . . . comfortably . . . and I want to speak to you about a matter of importance . . . important to you . . . and all I say to you . . . is for your benefit . . . everything you hear . . . will be positively placed in your mind . . . so that you are able to be more and more confident and comfortable about your exam . . .

On the day of the exam . . . you will be at ease with yourself . . . a nervous excitement will naturally appear . . . and you will be excited . . . knowing that you have the ability to do well in the exam . . . and . . . because you are sure in the knowledge that you have worked hard . . . learning what you needed to learn . . . you will be at ease with yourself . . . at ease with entering the exam room . . .

and at ease with the exam itself . . . and because you are at ease . . . you will have a focused concentration . . . a concentrated confidence . . . that reassures you that you are in control . . .

I want you to know that your confidence . . . will be enhanced because you will be confident about your ability in the exam . . . you will have a memory that has a natural recall . . . you already know that when you relax, you can recall what it is you want to recall . . . by relaxing for a moment . . . and as you relax . . . you will be able to ask your unconscious mind . . . to bring forward the information . . . you want it to bring forward . . . you are now sure in the knowledge that your memory has a natural recall . . . and you know the secret of how to trigger the recall . . . simply by relaxing for a moment and asking your unconscious mind to bring that information forward . . .

As soon as you start the exam, you will be totally at ease and focused . . . you will begin to read what it is you are to do . . . calmly and with a focused concentration . . . you will then plan how you will begin the exam steadily . . . you will perhaps take a few deep breaths to centre your concentration . . . or you may choose to begin planning your strategy straightaway . . . you plan your time . . . and recall all the facts that you already know . . . triggered by the exam question . . . you may decide to relax before you begin answering . . . and mentally ask your unconscious mind to retrieve information freely . . .

As you continue the exam . . . you remain completely at ease with yourself . . . your self-esteem and confidence strong ... your unconscious mind releasing all the information that you have learnt in preparation for the exam ... you even smile inside yourself, knowing how well you are doing ... sure in the knowledge that your steady approach to the exam ... is ensuring you are focused and concentrated ... your unconscious mind supporting you as it continues to release the information you want it to release ...

And all these things I say to you ... will happen exactly as I say ... they happen to you both inside and outside of this room ... you are now sure in the knowledge that your unconscious mind will release the information you need it to release for the exam ... you are now focused and at ease, sure in the knowledge that your memory will have a natural recall ... and you can be proud at how well you are working with your unconscious mind ... you can feel large helpings of self-esteem ... large helpings of self-confidence ... large helpings of relaxation, as you feel at ease with yourself ... the exam...and your ability to trigger a natural memory recall ...

Real Life

Alexandra

A 22-year—old, final-year business studies student, Alex had struggled with exam confidence throughout her school and student life. She understood that she had learnt the necessary methodologies, facts and case studies, but she really struggled to pull out the key facts and figures to use in her exam papers. In the past, she had tried going to cramming colleges and this had helped her to pass the exams she needed, but they left her exhausted and with the knowledge that she had to go elsewhere to find the confidence to perform successfully in exams.

As I talked to her, I knew that what Alexandra was really struggling with was developing a strategy for memory recall. As our initial session together progressed, we identified that Alexandra was a very visual person, so we developed an approach to exam preparation where Alexandra would use pictures and words to place and recall concrete facts. In addition to using pictures to recall facts, Alexandra decided she was really keen to use the relaxation and memory recall techniques.

As she began using these techniques, she said that she could pull out facts and figures with accuracy and confidence. By session two, Alexandra asked to use the stretch technique and wanted me to devise a little memory test that would mirror some of the exam conditions that had hampered her memory recall. Also during session two, I explained to Alex how the unconscious mind would help retrieve the most relevant information that she needed in the exam. Having done that, I then delivered a hypnotherapy session, using the script to help Alex set herself up in a focused, calm way for the final exams. She pointed out that the script would be a brilliant tool for her and said that she'd get her sister in on the act to read it while she focused on the relaxation it delivers.

In our third and final session, I had mocked-up an exam to test Alex's knowledge of the memory recall techniques that we had explored together and injected a bit of fun into it to help her come back to this when she needed it. I gave her half an hour to go through a paper of 20 questions based on what we had done together, and she scored 18 out of 20 to become my A student.

Alex was indeed a star student. She called me four months later to say, with great pride, that she had earned a first-class honours degree with a distinction in her exams. She was so confident of her exam ability that she decided to join a national firm and to go for qualifications to become a chartered accountant. Now that is daunting!

mitch

At 37, Mitch was desperate to become a qualified paramedic technician. After years of being involved in community groups and being the trained first aider, he wanted to take it up as a full-time, full-on career. The issue for Mitch, and the reason he came to see me, was that when it came to doing practical tests, he'd developed a phobia of people scrutinising him, to the point where he started to panic and forget his techniques.

My assessment was that he needed to get the phobia under control and let a vision of being a fully qualified paramedic be his goal, to keep the confidence with him at all times. Our four sessions together kicked off with an agreement to go for the 'ouch' point where Mitch felt that he wasn't able to demonstrate his skills and knowledge. Together we practised the stretch technique and that got Mitch testing his paramedic skills in front of the community group, against the clock and under close scrutiny. I also felt the mind game of building his own confidence room would be really useful in allowing him to store the feelings and sensations of successfully getting through the practical side of his paramedic exams.

In our final session together, Mitch and I worked on bringing some humorous references and images into what he had to do in his practical exam. Although he had the confidence to go for this serious, demanding and often very emotionally draining role, he needed to relax more to bring out the best in him during his exams. I won't go into the minutiae, but it involved mummies and tomato ketchup.

Mitch came out of the other end with a confidence room he could quickly slip into and come out of smiling inside, and with the capability to confidently perform the practical tasks required by his paramedic examiners. I'm delighted to say that he's the new number two in an ambulance team in Yorkshire, and he smiles like a Cheshire cat when he's doing the job he was born to do.

Tess

At 63, Tess had been married most of her adult life, but had lost her husband through cancer two years earlier. A wonderfully outgoing and seemingly confident woman, she had a dream that she wanted to fulfil — being able to drive her own car.

Tess's problem was that she felt she was too old to

learn, absorb and recall all the practical information and facts that people need to know to be able to pass the theory element of the driving test. She wasn't confident that she could take on board all the facts she needed in order to pass.

A friend referred Tess to me after she had failed the theory three times and was convinced that she couldn't get through it. I met with Tess for two sessions. During the first, we went through in detail my tips and advice for improving memory recall. We agreed that she needed to summarise, write down and arrange the information needed for the theory test, and that having a colour-coded system would help. We hit on the idea of traffic lights, with red, amber and green tied to specific areas. For example, danger and hazard information was linked to the red code.

We then decided that the other key to unlocking Tess's ability to confidently recall facts, images and numbers was linked to her ability to relax herself and know and feel she was confident in digging the information out. To do this, we practised the command and deliver technique, where Tess self-affirmed that she could keep the facts and information stored in her mind, but always available with stress-free recall and accuracy. I asked her to practise this daily for three weeks and to work on the script to improve memory recall.

Giving herself plenty of time, Tess went on to pass the theory element of the driving test on her fourth try and to nail the practical part to boot. She's now the proud owner of a bright red mini which she scoots around town in, visiting friends and family. Britain's worst driver — I don't think so!

Your secrets

- It is literally all in the mind, and you need to know how to relax the conscious mind to get out the information you need for exams and tests. Play the mind games.

- Use visual and audio tools, depending on your preferred way of exam cramming. For example, keep little cartoons that will draw you to particular parcels of written information and facts.

- Link key points you need to remember to jokes and humour or string them together into catchy rhyme.

- Keep putting it in and some of it will stick. The more you are able to write down and summarise the key facts that you need to retain, the easier they will become to recall.

Confident to Work for Yourself

Several years ago I decided to take the plunge and set up my own business. I called my boss and explained that I had decided to resign my position to set out into the business world.

This was a major step, and it felt as if I'd just walked on to a tightrope. At the time I was head of HR and training at a major media organisation. I was well paid, in a job that was very secure, and I had established strong, meaningful relationships with my colleagues. In a strange way, it had all become a bit too safe and it was time to start doing a bit of tightrope walking!

After several years in the role, I knew in my heart that it was time to move on, but time to move on to what? Did I want to move to a new organisation or did I want to go solo? I decided the latter was the right way to go because it would give me so many more options and give free rein to my energy and creativity.

On the practical side of things, I had weighed up the costs and benefits of both working for myself and working for someone else. Working for myself won the day because it gave me freedom and the potential to earn a lot more money (remember, you get out what you put in and most people who start out on their own don't get rich quick). But, of course, working for yourself isn't something you can or should rush into. There are many practical considerations to be made depending on your circumstances and what you want to do. As well as the boring but essential practicalities, you need to be prepared in your heart and mind. They have to both be on the same page and totally committed to what you are about to do. Be completely sure in the decision that setting up your own business is the right way to go.

So many considerations

Part of building your confidence to set out on the tightrope of starting your own business is to note and address all the practical considerations that might affect you. If you are really, really serious about running your own business, you are well advised to think through the following considerations:

1 Do you have a partner? If so, are they supportive? Will they be willing to take financial risks when needed to fund the business? Is their heart in it as much as yours? If yes, that is great. If not, forget it or accept that your relationship may come to a close.

2 Have you really got the self-belief needed to run your own business? Do you really believe in yourself, and the product that is you, enough to make your business dream turn into a reality? Do you really believe it or do you have some niggling self-doubt? If you aren't 100 per cent, forget it, because you will need to sell yourself confidently to a whole range of people, from your bank manager to prospective clients and customers. But if you totally believe in yourself, it should be all systems go – put the pedal to the metal!

3 Are you prepared to let go of the traditional 9–5 work routine, where you clock-watch and never give up your 'spare time'? So many naive people think that when you are master of your own ship you come and go as you please. Believe me, it doesn't quite work like that. You will probably work at least sixty hours per week, sometimes more, lose a lot of your holidays and your social life will take a leap off a cliff.

4 Have you prepared a cash-flow analysis? Try not to borrow from the bank, but if you do, keep any borrowing to a minimum. Borrowing isn't the end of the world and most businesses borrow to increase cash flow. Are you prepared for the risk this brings, especially if your house is secured against a business loan?

5 Do you really believe there is a demand for your product or service? Have you researched the market to check this out? If not, do so. You need to know there is a desire for your service or product before you go full steam ahead.

6 Is there a business plan in place? This should include the strategic objectives of your business, the tactical actions to achieve your objectives, a full assessment of what resources will be required to run the business and a projected cash-flow forecast. Draft the plan in that order and you will shine confidently in front of your bank manager.

Build the vision

Speak to any successful entrepreneur and they will tell you that having vision is a critical business attribute. You have to be able to paint a picture of what your business success will look and feel like. And then, of course, you need to be clear about what actions you need to take to make the vision a living reality. Use the clear goal model described on page 75 to help with this.

Clear outcome. What does the business look like, who are the customers, what's the brand, what does it feel like to do business with you? What does success look, feel, sound, smell and taste like? You might think it's daft to try to use your senses to pin down what your business success will be like but, believe me, this is all about building the solid foundations of your confidence to keep pushing the business forward, even when you hit problems, as all businesses inevitably do.

> You have to be able to paint a picture of what your business success will look and feel like

Consistent activities. What are you going to be doing month in, month out, week in, week out, day in, day out to help the business grow? Write these regular actions down and group them as monthly, weekly or daily activities, so that you have a clear focus on what you will be doing.

Immediate tasks. Having identified all the consistent activities that need to take place to turn the vision into a reality, it is now time to identify your top three immediate tasks. In other words, it is time to put the key into your ignition and hit the fire button!

Mind games

As well as considering the practical steps for setting up your business, it is also important to increase your confidence by programming your mind for success. By carrying out some of the mind games described in chapter 4, you will pre-programme your mind for business success. It is important to condition your mind at the unconscious level, so that the actions you take become habitual. Try using the soap opera and command and deliver mind games. If these aren't for you, try some of the others.

Copycat? It's crucial

Do you personally know any successful business people? If not, it's important to go out and find them. If you are struggling to think of successful entrepreneurs, try asking friends for recommendations or attend some decent networking events where top business people speak. Modelling how these people go about doing business can work miracles for your confidence. Find someone that inspires you by the way they sell their business to customers, the way they conduct themselves with customers, their creativity, their charisma, their organisation and financial skills. Don't be afraid to be nosey – just ask. Listen to what they say and model the bits that are missing for you. This really is a great way to become more confident. See them as your own personal business coach.

Of course, there are plenty of successful business people in the media who can be tapped into for inspiration and advice –

from Charles Dunstone, founder of the Carphone Warehouse, to lingerie entrepreneur Caprice. You can find out a lot about how they have done things and got through the tough times by doing some research on the internet.

Confidence with the bank manager

If you are meeting the bank manager to borrow money to fund your business, it's important to project the confidence that you have in yourself, your business and your future. Firstly, make sure you take along a business plan that includes all the elements outlined earlier. Secondly, brand yourself brilliant. Personal appearance is critical, so make sure you wear professional business attire and groom yourself to perfection. Remember, you are the face of the business and your bank manager will need to believe in you. Thirdly, before you go to the meeting, play some mind games to boost your confidence and make sure you go through your business plan with a friend to ensure you know it inside and out. Finally, when you meet the bank manager face to face, hold steady eye contact and show enthusiasm in your business plan. Take him or her through it carefully and be prepared to justify everything you have written.

The first year

Unless you have tapped into something big, don't expect a huge financial return in the first year, or the first few years. Normally, the first year is about nurturing and building the customer/ client base, as well as marketing and establishing a positive reputation. It can all seem a little scary at first, but with hard work, self-belief and emotional resilience, it will pay off. It really is important to keep affirming your self-belief as you begin running your business, and do be prepared to take the rough with the smooth. Most importantly, plan your marketing campaign carefully and do everything to look after your customers. My advice is to use internet marketing combined with a well-planned and executed public relations (PR) campaign if funds permit. And if business is quiet for a month or two, don't panic – this is all part of the economic and business cycles that we can't control. Instead, adopt the chill tips described in chapter 3 and stay positive.

Going back to a salaried job

It is important to remember that if you decide to run your own business, you will develop new skills, knowledge and attitudes that any future employer will see as positive. Running your own business will mean you will develop commercial acumen, creativity, decision-making skills, organisational skills, emotional resilience and financial awareness, all of which are key competencies demanded by many companies of all sizes. Thousands of people return to full-time employment after a spell of running their own small businesses, so remember, if you decide you've had enough of being your own boss or things get sticky, you do have an option to return to being employed. Don't allow this to destroy your confidence; instead, let it do the opposite and look at it as a fresh adventure and a new challenge. You are an excellent product that someone will snap up to make a difference to their business.

> Look at it as a fresh adventure and a new challenge

Be confident to build your own business: the script

The following script is designed to embed positive suggestions into your mind so that you can boost your confidence to start your own business. To use the script, sit comfortably in a quiet, warm room, place your hands on your thighs, relax deeply by letting all your muscles become heavy and tired and then count down slowly from ten to one. Once you are relaxed, slowly read the script to yourself. Alternatively, you may ask someone to read the script to you slowly, as you relax comfortably with your eyes closed. If you choose to do this, it is best to signal that you are ready to begin by lifting one of your index fingers rather than speaking out loud, so that your relaxation isn't disturbed. Notice that there are intervals between certain words to help ensure the script sinks deep into your mind.

And as you sit ... reflecting and relaxing as you do ... I want you to know that ... as you sit there comfortably ... you can take a few deep breaths ... and as you breathe out ... you breathe out any unnecessary nervous tension ... which helps you to relax even deeper ... and deeper ... relaxed ... so that you become more and more ... completely at ease with yourself ...

As you take each deep breath, I want you to become aware ... as you let go ... as you let go of all the unnecessary tension ... that you feel more at ease ... more comfortable and relaxed ... both physically and mentally at ease ... so much so that these things I say to you ... drift deeper and deeper into your mind ... more and more progressively ... more and more deeply ...

I want you to know that as you rest . . . listening to the things I say to you . . . these things I do say to you . . . will sink deeper and deeper into your mind . . . all for your benefit . . . supporting your confidence to become . . . stronger and more focused . . . helping you to make that move to start your business . . . your confidence will take a boost . . . because these things I say to you . . . will increase your confidence immediately . . .

You are now very aware of these things I say to you . . . and I want you to know that the concerns you have right now . . . the concerns you have are quite natural . . . because our instinct as human beings is to survive . . . and you have until this moment felt that stepping out of your comfort zone . . . has threatened your survival . . . and that is all, of course, quite natural . . . because you are moving into unknown territory . . . and when we move into unknown territory we naturally become concerned for our own survival . . .

I want you to know that all of this is quite natural . . . but you can become confident . . . knowing that you are focused . . . you have your vision in place . . . the outcome is set and you know all that it is you have to do to make it happen . . . you are confident because you understand that no business is guaranteed success . . . but because you have the drive . . . the motivation . . . the focus on what it is you have to do . . . you are confident that your business will be the success . . . you want your business to be . . .

You are feeling focused . . . more motivated . . . driven and enthused, as you know your business will be the success you want it to be . . . and because you are excited about running your business . . . you can be confident that you are already a success . . . you understand that doing all the things you need to do for your business . . . will drive your business to be the success you know it can be . . . and you are now feeling more confident . . . because you know that working hard...with the focus and energy that you have . . . you will be a success . . .

It's as though you are now putting things into perspective . . . you understand there are all kinds of risks in life . . . it is, of course, natural to appreciate the risks of setting up your own business . . . but for you . . . you are now confident that with the focus . . . motivation . . . hard work . . . and drive . . . it will be the success you want it to be . . . you feel excited . . . relaxed . . . sure in the knowledge that . . . you will now move forward . . . confident . . . confident that you are doing this . . . as you know you are confident . . . focused with the vision clearly in your mind . . . confident to be successful running your own business . . .

Real Life

Claire

Claire left her last job not because of the money, but because of the drag of the commute and because she really didn't enjoy the work she was doing. Basically, she was becoming downhearted and miserable and felt it just wasn't worth it. She decided to quit her job and, with a month's salary in the bank and lots of bills to pay, to set up on her own as a self-employed marketing consultant.

Claire managed okay, but then decided to have a baby. Working as long as she could, she was only eligible to £400 per month statutory maternity pay. She took just a few weeks off work when her daughter was born, just at the time the credit crunch started to hit. Fortunately, her husband's salary covered the mortgage, some bills and the food shopping. In between caring for her daughter and trying to get back on track, Claire was thinking about her future. She loved marketing work, but her income was wholly dependent on her time and she was marketing other people's businesses. Claire wanted something of her own to market! One day she was chatting to her friend Kate and they decided to set up in business together. But they needed a product that was going to fit around their busy lives. To work for them, it needed to be web-based, feature an online shop, involve products which were small enough to easily store and ship and yet of high value, be in an emerging market where they could become big fish, be something where they could offer great customer service, have minimal start-up costs and finally, and importantly, be something they would enjoy.

Many texts later, Claire received one saying 'men's make-up' from Kate, and they knew that was it. They worked out some figures, put a business plan together as best they could, got a bit of funding from Business Link for a website and started trading. The vision was to become big players in the industry. They knew that there would be lots of challenges with this business. It was not an easy idea to sell in the UK, where a few years ago even moisturiser for men was considered emasculating. They knew they'd have to find some excellent products and just go for it. So they did. Since then they have made over DJ Scott Mills live on the Radio One webcam and they have made many contacts, including US President Barack Obama's make-up artist.

Claire and Kate are loving what they do. The business is still young, but is growing month on month and they're aiming for £200k turnover within the next two years. Claire explains that if she hadn't taken the risk of leaving her job, she would never have known if she could make it on her own. She knew she could always find another job if it didn't work, but was determined not to use that option. Claire thinks that if you spend your life waiting for the 'right time' to go it alone, it will never come. Claire did it the right way. She did her research, got organised, had the vision clearly established in her mind and went for it! There are so many recipes for successful businesses. Claire came to the new venture with the firm self-belief that she would be doing something that she loved and was completely passionate about, so both she and Kate threw themselves into it. If you believe in what you're doing, it will come across to others — enthusiasm is infectious. Hard work helps, speaking to other business owners is good too, but at the end of the day, there is no substitute for getting on and actually doing it.

David

At the age of 34, David faced a life-threatening illness. Working as a pharmacist in London, he decided to return to Arbroath in Scotland, to be close to his family. At the same time, realising just how serious his illness was, David decided to take time out and travel to Brazil, where he enjoyed a spiritual healing retreat that helped him re-evaluate his life. Soon after David returned home, he was admitted to hospital, where he came close to losing his life. David remained in hospital for almost a month and upon leaving decided the best course of action would be to just be with his loved ones. The experience of coming close to death meant David's perspective on life changed. Health and well-being were now David's core values and working for someone else again was not on his agenda. He realised life was too short and wanted to live his life on his own terms, doing what really inspired him.

With a passion for personal development, David decided that he would train to become a life coach. He enrolled in one of the UK's top life-coaching schools and, having successfully completed his training, immediately set up his own practice and built up a client base. David now divides his time between life coaching and working as a self-employed pharmacist, and his business continues to grow.

Well aware of the confidence issues people have when it comes to setting up their own business, he believes that if the desire is strong enough, you will find a way to make the business flourish. In conversations with David, he describes three components to making a new business succeed. Firstly, he explains that any new business needs a vision that truly inspires and excites you, that brings out your passions, so that you know where you are going and what has to be done to get there. Secondly, he notes that you have to have the determination to succeed and believe that you will be successful. Lastly, he says you need to implement a logical plan that is time-bound.

Interestingly, David also believes customers can be drawn to a new business using the law of attraction. To attract customers, David recommends the business owner thinks and feels successful at all times and lets go of resistance, rather than allowing negative thoughts to sabotage your personal and business success. He says that we all use our minds to think, so we may as well make sure that what we do think is positive and life-enhancing.

Ray

Ray was made redundant from his job in the public sector after working for a local authority for over 20 years. At 45, he thought his usefulness in the workplace was over and told me when we first met that he'd never taken such a blow to his confidence before and was totally lost about how to get back on his feet.

I explained to Ray that to move forward he needed to get his head straight and he agreed to adopt several of the mind games to bring this part of his confidence machine back into working order. He started with command and deliver and went on to really enjoy working on the fine fusion technique, to bring back the many times he'd felt really confident and use them to move forward.

As we talked, it became clear that Ray had a lifelong

ambition of opening an antiques shop in a country town, but he'd kept filling his own head with negative thoughts that told him it wasn't possible, he wasn't clever enough, he couldn't risk his financial security, and so on. Talking through things, it became clear that the only thing holding Ray back was Ray. He had the money in the bank to start up and still had part of a public sector pension to tide him over in the future.

I helped Ray to practically plan what he needed to do to launch his own antiques business, from drawing up a priorities checklist to having a look at his business plan. Ray assured me that he was ready to go for his dream and that he felt in his heart and his mind that this was an opportunity he had to take.

Ray keeps in contact with me and I've visited his 'curiosity' shop in Yorkshire on more than one occasion, to see Ray the proud and confident owner of his own little business.

7 Secrets of Confidence

- Use the clear goal model to help develop a clear business strategy.

- Use the mind games to build belief in yourself.

- Prepare a projected cash-flow forecast.

- Ensure that you ooze confidence and charisma and know your business idea/model inside out when you go to visit the bank manager.

- If it feels right in your heart and head, that is your unconscious mind telling you to go for it.

Confident About Your Weight

It probably comes as no surprise that millions of people complain of low levels of self-esteem and confidence because they feel they are too fat. We all know that waistlines are continuing to expand and the obesity time-bomb has already started to explode, especially in the USA and the UK. Having worked with hundreds of clients over the years, supporting them to lose weight, I can, from first-hand experience, confirm that there is a direct correlation between being too fat and having low self-worth. But repairing confidence in this area needs personal responsibility, self-motivation and a good dollop of mind-programming. The aim is quite simply to adopt a mindset and lifestyle that is conducive to having your body beautiful.

Weight off your mind:
check your body image and *checklist*
confidence

1   Do people positively comment on the way you look?

2   When you look in the mirror are you happy with what
you see?

3   Can you buy the clothes that you really want to?

4   Do you often think people look at you too critically?

5   Are you confident you eat sensibly and don't let your
emotions take over when it comes to food choices?

6   If you are overweight, are you happy with your body and
soul?

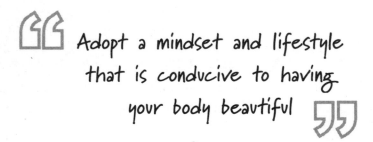

Adopt a mindset and lifestyle
that is conducive to having
your body beautiful

No excuses – let them go!

Excuses are the demons that prevent you from losing weight. So
many people stay overweight because they say they will start to
lose weight tomorrow, only to find tomorrow never comes. The
excuses are plentiful, with top of the poll being: 'It's difficult to
lose weight as you get older.' To let go of the excuses, begin by

writing them all down and once you have done this agree with yourself that these excuses belong in the past. Use one of the techniques described in chapter 1 to help you let go of the excuses, so that you can begin to move forward today. It really is only once you have taken care of the excuses that you can move on and shrink down.

I'm sure some of you reading this will have the impish little demons whispering in your ear: 'You're not fit enough to lose weight,' 'Big bones won't let you shed the flab,' and so on. I'm going to teach you how to confidently shove that impish excuse-maker into the nothingness where it belongs.

Mind your weight

Mind games are a critical part of long-term weight control. It isn't just about losing the weight in order to feel confident; it's also about keeping it off so your confidence continues to grow. If you want to feel confident about your weight, it is going to be essential to programme your mind to achieve your goal at the unconscious level. It is then, and only then, that you will become automatically in control of your eating habits, your exercise regime and your motivation levels. Try using the following three-week mind-programming strategy to help turn yourself around from feeling down about your weight to feeling super confident that not only are you shedding the pounds, but you now have absolute control over where your weight is going for the long haul.

Week 1: Soap opera

In deep relaxation, see, hear and feel yourself at your ideal weight. Pay attention to what you are wearing and how good it feels to be slim, trim and free from fat. Notice people around you staring with admiring eyes, and hear the positive comments as people pay you compliments. Also, pay attention to what you are saying to yourself, such as, 'It feels great to be in control of my eating habits' and 'I feel great knowing I can wear whatever I want to wear.' Do this at least twice a day for the first seven days of your mind-programming strategy, as this will embed the weight goal into your unconscious mind. You will feel your confidence grow as you practise this technique.

Week 2: Command and deliver

During week two, it is important to affirm that you have complete control over your eating habits as well as other associated activities, such as exercise and self-discipline. Having completed the soap opera technique, your mind now has the weight goal firmly embedded at the unconscious level. Now you can move on to affirm the actions you will take to achieve the goal and maintain it. Construct strong positive commands such as 'I am in control of my eating habits' and 'I am confident and focused to lose the spare tyre.' As you mentally say these commands to yourself, turn up the volume and increase the feelings of motivation as you hear them sink deep into your mind.

Week 3: Dissociate and reintegrate

In week three, use the dissociate and reintegrate mind game described on page 76 to remind your mind that you have let go of the things you once did that kept you overweight, and have now brought in new habits conducive to weight control. Do this at least once a day, so that your mind continues to programme itself at the unconscious level. Another way of putting it is to understand that your mind understands that you have dumped the old overweight you and fallen in love with the new slimmer you.

Motivate yourself

To help yourself to lose weight, it is critical that you become self-motivated. If you sit around thinking it will never happen, then it never will. Lifting your motivation will ensure you get your backside into action and start shedding the pounds. Use the following ten tips to help trigger instant motivation:

1 Tough love. Set yourself a goal and if you fail to meet it, punish yourself. For example, if you set a goal to lose eight pounds in weight over a four-week period and only lose six, then perhaps give yourself some tough love by not going out socially for the following month. Remember, motivation isn't just about carrots; sticks also play their part. Conversely, if you achieve the goal, reward yourself – but not with carrot cake!

2 Keep the end result in sight. Make sure you keep visualising the end result, seeing, hearing and feeling yourself slim, trim and confident. If it helps, try drawing a picture that represents the end result and look at it daily.

3 Take a photograph. Go into the bathroom and take a photograph of yourself in your underwear. Let this remind you of what you currently look like and allow it to motivate you to slim down to a body beautiful.

4 Pin up new clothes. Go out and buy an item of clothing in a smaller size. Put this somewhere you will see it daily and let it be your motivator.

5 Clear out the cupboards. Go and clear out the junk food from your cupboards and pay attention to how it makes you feel powerful and confident as you slam them into the bin.

6   Stop, look and listen. When you find yourself about to grab unhealthy food from the fridge or the supermarket shelf, stop and think for a few moments. Then remember what it is you want to look like. Do you really have to have this food? Will it benefit you? Will it help you achieve your goal? If the answer is 'no', see a bright-red STOP sign in your mind. Then reach for some healthy food instead and realise just how in control of your eating habits you are.

7   Get a buddy. If you have a friend who is equally lacking confidence due to their size, it is often a good idea to team up. There are many things you can do together, such as setting the weight-loss goals, food shopping, going for walks, as well as motivating each other to stay focused on the end result.

8   Be dramatic. If you are a natural extrovert, be dramatic and shout out loud your plans to lose weight. Tell all your friends and be excited as you confirm this is the time to shrink down. Declaring your weight-loss plans can be really positive, as it affirms your intentions.

9   Flirt again. If it floats your boat, keep reminding yourself how easy it will be to flirt again. Imagine bumping into an ex who dumped you and treated you like crap and seeing

the look of desire in his or her eyes, only for you to have the satisfaction of knowing that no matter how much they want you, it's just too late.

10 JFDI – Just Flipping Do It! Are you a talker or a doer? Think right now of those people you know who do nothing but talk about doing something rather than actually getting on and doing it. Do you want that to be you?

Copycat

If you are able to identify someone who has lost weight and is now in control of their weight, do play the copycat game described in chapter 7. Observe what they do and, if you know them personally, discuss openly how they successfully maintain their ideal weight. Remember in your observation to identify how your role model behaves around food, the attitudes they have towards weight control and the beliefs they affirm to themselves to maintain a healthy lifestyle.

> " Identify someone who has lost weight and is now in control of their weight "

Be confident about your weight: the script

The following script is designed to embed positive suggestions into your mind so that you increase your confidence to lose weight. To use the script, sit comfortably in a quiet, warm room, place your hands on your thighs, relax deeply by letting all your muscles become heavy and tired and then count down slowly from ten to one. Once you are relaxed, slowly read the script to yourself. You can also ask someone to read the script to you slowly, as you relax comfortably with your eyes closed. If you choose to do this, it is best to signal that you are ready to begin by lifting one of your index fingers rather than speaking out loud, so that your relaxation isn't disturbed. Notice that there are intervals between certain words to help ensure the script sinks deep into your mind.

As you relax ... more and more deeply ... I want you to imagine a peaceful scene ... this can be somewhere you know well or somewhere you have dreamt of ... and ... you can feel the relaxation spreading throughout your body ... as you sink deeper and deeper ... deeper into that wonderful state of both physical and mental relaxation ...

In your place of relaxation ... you can begin to allow all the muscles of your body to become ... more and more rested ... more and more tired ... because you know that you are safe and at ease ... in your place ... seeing what you see ... hearing what you hear ... and feeling what you feel ... and I want you to know that in a few moments ... in a few moments' time ... you will hear me count down from ten to one ...

I want you to know that . . . with each number . . . each number between ten and one . . . you will become one-tenth more relaxed . . . each number . . . will help you drift . . . all the way down into a deep state of complete physical as well as mental relaxation . . . that will . . . help you relax more and more completely . . . and as I count . . . down from ten to one . . . you will drift anywhere you like . . .

As you drift . . . my voice will go with you . . . as I speak to your unconscious mind . . . about something important to you . . . so ready . . . ten . . . nine . . . eight . . . going deeper and deeper into a calm . . . relaxed . . . and comfortable state . . . seven . . . six . . . more and more relaxed . . . five . . . four . . . three . . . more relaxed now . . . two . . . and one . . . all the way down relaxed . . . and you can relax twice as much . . . as I speak to your unconscious mind about an important matter . . . important to you . . .

And as I speak to your unconscious mind . . . these things I say to you . . . will happen exactly as I tell you they will happen . . . all for your benefit . . . you told me that you wanted to . . . lose weight . . . and because it is your wish to . . . lose weight . . . so you will begin to . . . lose weight . . . and in your mind right now . . . I want you to see yourself at your ideal weight . . . right now . . . see . . . hear . . . feel . . . yourself at your ideal weight . . . notice what you wear . . . what you are saying to yourself . . . what you feel . . . now that you are at your ideal weight . . .

At your ideal weight you notice how good it feels . . . to feel so slim . . . and trim . . . I want you to see . . . hear . . .

and feel yourself slim...trim...in control...pay attention to what you look like now you are lighter...the compliments people pay to you...the positive things you say to yourself...feel how confident you feel...now that you are lighter...slimmer and trimmer...see what you see...hear what you hear...feel what you feel...

And as you listen to my voice...I am now speaking directly to your unconscious mind...and I am going to suggest a number of things...actions...habits...that you will carry out...because you know that these are all for your benefit...helping you to be a ... slimmer...trimmer...fitter...you...what I suggest to you...these actions will happen exactly as I tell you they will happen...both inside...and outside of this room...

I am going to suggest to your unconscious mind...that you have no desire to eat sickly sweet and fatty foods ...that you are in control of your eating habits...you have no desire to eat fatty foods...no desire to eat fatty foods...and because it is your wish to reject...fatty foods...sickly sweet foods...this is why you are reducing your weight...and...you are reducing your weight...the fat is melting...easily...

You have no desire to eat fatty foods...and you reject fatty foods...and you will always be pleased when you reject...fatty foods...in fact, it won't be long before you find...fatty and sweet foods...bland and taste-less...and you have no desire to eat fatty foods...no matter where you are...at home...at work...when travelling...when socialising...you have no desire to eat fatty foods...

You will also begin to notice that you eat smaller amounts ... as your stomach shrinks ... you notice that you have no desire to eat fatty foods ... as your stomach shrinks ... and because your stomach is shrinking ... you eat smaller amounts ... and you eat the right kind of food ... healthy, nutritious food ... and as your stomach is now shrinking, you eat slowly ... chew every mouthful of healthy, nutritious food ... you pause as you eat ... and you will feel comfortably full ... now that your stomach is shrinking ...

You will know soon you will achieve your goal ... and because you are sure in the knowledge that you will reach your goal ... you now feel so driven ... motivated ... energised ... because you are shrinking ... the fat is melting ... your stomach shrinking ... you know that you are reducing your weight naturally ... the weight loss is step by step ... little by little as the unnecessary fatty tissues continue to melt away ... feel it right now as the fatty tissues melt away ...

And as the days ... weeks ... and months go by, you will remain in control of your eating habits ... your stomach will continue to shrink ... you will see ... hear ... feel yourself slimmer ... trimmer ... fitter ... altogether you will shrink and reach your weight goal ... easily and effortlessly ... and your life will be so much more satisfying ... satisfying to you ...

Real Life

Brenda

I met Brenda, 55, in December 2006. She contacted me seeking support to lose four stones in weight, and at the time she looked miserable and completely fed up with life. She straightforwardly said that she wanted to look and feel good again and had tried everything possible to lose weight, including most commercial diets and dozens of celebrity DVDs.

Pushing away rigid diets, I agreed with Brenda that the goal was to achieve a long-term lifestyle change. I decided to work with Brenda over a three-week period, to help condition her mind for long-term weight control. During the first week, I used direct-suggestion hypnotherapy sessions and delivered straight-talking advice to kick-start Brenda's journey towards a weight she would feel comfortable with. I also directed Brenda to place visible affirmations around the house and instructed her to go out and buy a pair of jeans a few sizes too small and hang them on the wardrobe door in the bedroom. In week two, Brenda agreed to step up the exercise habit and increase her exercise by walking an extra forty-five minutes a day. In addition, I delivered two sessions of clinical hypnotherapy, utilising the soap opera and command and deliver mind games. Finally, in week three, Brenda stepped up her motivation by digging out old photographs of herself looking like a stranded hippo to remind herself what she was leaving behind.

During the final week, I also delivered a session of hypnotherapy, using the weight-loss script.

Brenda had successfully turned her life around in

three weeks and went on to lose four stones in weight. She can be seen pounding the pavements around her home, as she got the bug for exercise, especially power-walking, which she says has given her a new lease of life.

Charlotte

At eighteen and a half stone, Charlotte was an unhappy young woman. She was married with no children and ran her own mortgage-broking business. Having read about the success of one of my clients in a glossy magazine, she contacted me, desperate for help to lose weight.

The desperation in her voice is something that will always stick with me, as she emotionally explained how she had attempted numerous diets and had at best lost a stone. It was becoming apparent that the reason Charlotte was so fat was because she had no motivation to lose weight and her focus on the mountainous task was just not there.

I knew from the word go that tea and tissues were not going to help Charlotte to shed the lard, so I developed a three-week plan of straight-talking motivation. It really was simple: Charlotte was fat because she was lazy and had no real intention of losing weight. She would rather eat an ice cream than an apple, sit on the couch all evening watching TV as opposed to taking a walk, and moan about how difficult it was to shift the flab rather than creating a motivated and realistic plan of action. Allowing Charlotte to cry into her doughnut would only make things worse, although she might not have scoffed the soggy doughnut.

During the first week, we walked together and talked,

examining all the excuses she had made, and agreed to shred them. Charlotte was told in no uncertain terms that if she didn't get her backside into action, she would stay fat and probably develop some serious health issues. I quickly went on to deliver a session of authoritarian clinical hypnotherapy and she agreed to chuck out all the junk food, develop her own menu using common sense and develop an exercise plan, to include a one-hour walk each day, which we would build on.

During week two, Charlotte used the clear goal model mind game to help programme her mind to focus on the end result. I also informed Charlotte that she was to increase her exercise to include an hour's walk in the morning, as well as the hour-long walk in the evening. She agreed to do this, with a lot of reluctance.

By week three, Charlotte was showing the first real signs of natural determination and motivation. I encouraged her to get tough with herself when needed and reward herself if she deserved it. She explained that she would look into the mirror and remind herself that the days of being a fat lard-arse had gone; excuses had been kicked into nothing. In Charlotte's words, it was 'time to stop looking for the answers in the fridge and go for a walk'.

Charlotte went on to lose a total of seven stones in weight and has successfully maintained her new shape. Charlotte's success was down to a big injection of tough love, learning to get excited and motivated about weight loss and using mind games to programme herself to shrink. I think what really helped her was having someone from the outside looking in (that's me) and telling her honestly that she was a fat mess who could pick her self-respect and self-confidence back up by starting to exercise and eat sensibly. She had to believe she could do it and allow me to help her to get rid of the wicked imps of self-doubt.

Sarah

Being a surrogate mum for a friend was the reason that Sarah had become fat, or so she told me when we met. She blamed her overweight body 100 per cent on giving birth, and made every excuse possible for being clinically obese. Not only did she live on junk food, she would spend virtually all her free time sitting on the sofa, claiming she was exhausted from looking after her own children. At five feet two inches, Sarah weighed in at over 15 stone and the flab spilled out of her size 18 clothes; in her own words, it was 'not a pretty sight'.

But one day, having had enough of feeling constantly drained and too fat, Sarah decided to take personal responsibility to begin shedding the lard. On recommendation from one of her friends, she decided to seek my advice and found it in one of my other titles, namely *Get Off Your Arse and Lose Weight*. Sarah told me she spent a number of nights reading what she had to do, including digging a photo out of herself that created an aversion to being fat, buying a dress a size smaller to motivate her, developing an exercise routine that fitted into her busy life and ditching the sugar- and fat-rich junk food that she had become hooked on.

Sarah then got in touch with me directly and I helped her to master several mind games, utilising the soap opera technique and keeping the end result in sight. She also gave herself stacks of tough love to ensure she remained on track and determined to achieve her desired goal. Sarah's attitude had turned around into a confident, positive one, having ditched the excuses and built in the JFDI mantra into her personal philosophy on weight loss. Sarah appeared with me on local television in 2009, showing off her new gorgeous shape. She really is a true inspiration to all other women who are looking to reduce their weight having given birth to their children. After bringing a brood of three babies into the world, Sarah is living proof that it can be done. That's another major excuse used to knock self-confidence that's gone.

Bill

Bill was an unusual client when it came to weight loss and obesity because when he turned up, all 22 stones of him, at our meeting, he showed me photographs of himself just five years earlier, when he'd been a super-fit infantry corporal. He'd boxed for the army and was always out in front when his boys were speed-marching and so on.

Meeting Bill, who was 38, and seeing his soldiering snaps, you'd be forgiven for thinking that he really was a 'mountain of his former self'. I needed to find out what had happened to turn Bill from an iron man into a tub of wobbly fat. As expected, it was a slide into self-loathing and depression, and he told me it had been brought about by a combination of being medically discharged from the forces and coming back and finding that his wife, the love of his life, had been playing away from home. She ditched him, saying he wasn't what she'd married.

Bill reacted to these horrible events in his life by turning to booze and food to fill the gaps. He'd almost daily be sinking 10–15 pints of lager and would stuff his face with kebabs, pizzas and crisps. Fortunately, he'd turned a corner after waking up passed out on a mate's floor and, looking in the mirror, didn't recognise the guy who was looking back at him, nor did he like him. He came to me after someone told him I could help him to get his mind back into shape and give him the motivation to make sure that his body followed suit.

In the first week, we agreed that we needed to build up his self-confidence and get his head straight and focused on the goal that would bring back his self-respect, i.e. the weight loss. Bill was a quick learner and picked up a series of mind games that allowed him to get back on track.

During the second week, Bill and I agreed on some of the practical steps that he could take to help speed up weight loss, such as ditching all the junk food in his cupboards, throwing away the takeaway menus, working out a healthy-eating plan and starting to exercise again. The latter was probably the toughest step for a guy who'd been used to physically leading others from the front and now had to start right from the bottom, with daily walks.

Once he'd clearly put his mind to turning things around and he'd started to claw back his confidence and self-belief, Bill started to shed the pounds faster than a one-armed bandit. It was a rewarding experience to see him, just eight months later, weighing in at a healthy and respectable 14 stones. He's now out there, dating and working in an inspiring role with a youth offending team.

7 Secrets of Confidence

Your secrets

- Write down all the excuses you have used for being fat. Take a look at them and make a pledge to ditch them by ripping up the piece of paper.

- Play some mind games to help condition the unconscious mind to lose weight.

- Identify what motivates you to lose weight and then Just Flipping Do It (JFDI).

- Get a weight-loss buddy to support you and steer clear of so-called friends who say you look okay the way you are – they are jealous drains.

- Use the weight-loss script daily and get hold of my other motivational book and common-sense guide to weight loss – *Get Off Your Arse and Lose Weight*.

Confident Sports Performance

The increased competitiveness of sports can make sports professionals react in a manner that may negatively affect their performance. For example, they may become tense, self-doubting, worry about the outcome of the competition and find it immensely difficult to be focused. To be at the top of your game in any sport, you need real confidence and a vision that you are going to win. Without confidence, or with diminished self-confidence, then athletes and sportspeople will under-perform.

Building self-confidence will help to crush natural competitive anxiety and maintain high levels of performance. In fact, all of the 7 Secrets can be applied directly to improving and maintaining confidence in sport. Over the years, I have supported a range of top sports professionals, ranging from golfers to footballers to sprinters, and I have consistently applied each of the secrets to help them build their confidence and get on top of their game.

> To be at the top of your game in any sport, you need real confidence and a vision that you are going to win

Let go of past failures

It can be so easy to sit around and reflect on the times when you have lost a race, competition or game, but doing so will simply reinforce failure. A classic example has to be the England cricket team, who continue to snatch defeat from the jaws of victory because as individuals and, it would seem, as a team they let their confidence levels fall, reflecting on previous setbacks or defeats. When they win, they display real professionalism, but all too often they seem to be influenced by negatives that have happened in the past.

Letting go of the times when your performance didn't quite hit the winning heights you'd wished for helps remove self-doubt and clears the path for a new winning streak. Give yourself permission to let go and affirm that the past is now past. If it helps, try writing down the negative past experiences, tear them up and bin them. This will help you to move forward with a fresh mind and focus on a successful outcome in your competitive arena.

If you do find that your mood is affected by a negative experience and self-doubt starts to creep in, try out some of the following exercises to snap out of it:

- Use positive thinking and suggestion, saying to yourself, 'I feel good' or 'I am going to move faster' or 'I am confident and in control and I will make the winning play.' Affirming this will help.

- Treat each part of your performance separately. When mistakes are made, simply refocus and concentrate on the next, separate part of the performance where you have done something really well.

- Use imagery (soap opera). Try imagining a relaxed scene or think back to a time when you performed well and re-experience how good it felt.

- Look at your goals and review them to help motivate yourself.

- Smile! Yes, force yourself to smile for a minute. It is impossible to feel moody and dwell on failure when you are smiling!

- Kick yourself up the backside and tell yourself to quit being moody and get on with it. A little tough love on yourself can work wonders.

Perfection breeds problems

Perfectionism in sport can lead to increased states of anxiety. Perfectionism will not only make you become tense and agitated, but it can also increase self-doubt and ultimately poor performance. Of course, I'm not suggesting you sit back on your laurels, thinking it will just happen; no such thing. Instead, it's important to recognise that you will, of course, develop a plan to perform at your best, but accept that as a fallible human being, if mistakes happen, you are still a worthwhile individual. The less you are in a struggle with yourself, striving for perfection, the better you will perform. Just remember, you want to perform to the best of your ability and push it a bit beyond if you can. If you do this, you can't ask for anything more from yourself and those around you will recognise that you are a winner.

Relax and win

Relaxation is a useful tool to help sports people rest, recover and relieve muscular tension. Equally important, relaxation will promote a clear mental state to aid the mind games described in chapter 4, which are critical in helping to increase self-belief and establish mental alertness prior to warming up for a competition.

One of the most difficult obstacles for sports people to overcome is anxiety. Anxiety can become even more of an obstacle when the sport requires intense concentration, such as golf. Anxiety may also be triggered by competition-related stress, such as relationships with other team members, and other factors outside the sporting event, such as insomnia. Relaxation techniques can prove very useful in alleviating anxiety in sport. The two most common types of relaxation techniques are progressive relaxation and imagination relaxation. Progressive relaxation is characterised by relaxing each muscle group, mentally counting down from ten to one and affirming a relaxed state, whereas imaginative relaxation techniques utilise creative visualisation. Ensure you use a range of the chill tips described in chapter 3 to ensure both your physical and mental state is fit to achieve gold.

Programme a winning mind

The power of your mind is as important as the state of your physical fitness. Take as examples inspiring athlete Linford Christie, who used the power of his mind to help him sharpen his edge to achieve gold, and former javelin champion Tessa Sanderson, whose mind focus was evident on the field. As former top tennis star David Lloyd explains, 'It's better to have a strong mind than natural talent; 80 per cent of the game is in the mind.' No doubt you will have heard many times sports commentators talking about teams and individuals who lost the game or their battle because their minds were not on the competition or game in hand.

> " It's better to have a strong mind than natural talent; 80 per cent of the game is in the mind "

There are a number of specific mind-programming techniques that will help increase self-confidence. You will find that you will prefer some techniques over others. Practise each to find out what suits you best.

1) Mind goals. Goal-setting is used by top-level athletes and business people alike. Processing goals in the mind will give you vision and motivation. Goals are what drive successful sports people, helping to focus time and resources in order to achieve. See, hear and feel these goals in your mind, as well as writing them out. Above all, get excited about these goals by turning up the feelings of excitement and enthusiasm. Make sure that you set your goals positively and keep them short, precise and to the point, rather than a heap of waffle, by making them outcome and time based, such as increasing the speed of the tennis ball when you serve to 20mph by 1 December 2010. And, of course, if you end up with a number of goals, set priorities, so that you don't feel overwhelmed. Above all, make sure that they are achievable, so you can experience progress towards achieving them. Once the goals are established, embed them in deep relaxation, seeing, hearing and feeling the achievement of them.

2) Soap opera. Using imagery is critical in the world of sport. It is the process by which the sports person can create and strengthen unconscious conditioning to perform well in sport. Imagery can be particularly useful to sports people who are injured and cannot train in any other way, or perhaps when the correct equipment isn't available and when rapid practice is required. But imagery (the soap opera technique) has additional applications to help support confidence in sport.

- It allows you to practise and prepare for unexpected events and circumstances. Imagery will allow you to enter a number of situations you have never physically experienced before with the feeling that you have been there before and accomplished whatever you are trying to achieve.

- Imagery also allows you to prepare and practise your response to physical and psychological problems that do not usually occur, so that you can respond to them confidently if they do occur. Lots of unexpected things can happen in sport, especially opponents not doing what they 'normally' do; for example, if you are playing someone at tennis who's always been weak on their backhand and you are thrashed by an awesome series of backhand strokes. If you can picture what may happen before it does, you'll be ready with a winning answer.

- Using imagery to pre-experience the achievement of goals is also powerful. It helps to give you confidence that these goals can be achieved, and will allow you to increase your abilities to levels you might not otherwise have reached. Just imagine, for example, a high-jumper who needs to push beyond their personal best. It's simple: they see the bar being raised to break a national record or world record. It really is a case of 'seeing is believing' and if you are believing then you can do it.

- Imagery also helps you to slow down and play out in your mind difficult and complex skills, ensuring that you set your mind up to use the skills competently. This will help mind and body to work together.

When using imagery, ensure that you have a strong image, as opposed to a weak one. This will be much more effective in conditioning your unconscious mind. Do make sure that you use all your senses when utilising the imagery technique, including touch, sound, smell, taste and feelings. This can be further enhanced by focusing on specific sensations, such as the feeling of gripping a bat, the roar of the crowd, the shape of the stadium, the texture of your sports kit and even the smell of your own sweat! Try to associate yourself with your image by imagining yourself within your body and noticing all that is going on around you, as opposed to looking at yourself from a distant position.

3) Focus and flow. These are at the heart of building confidence and achievement in sports performance. In summary, focus is giving your complete attention to the execution of your sports skills, and flow is a state of being completely focused and engrossed in the execution of a sports performance, to the complete exclusion of everything else. When experiencing a state of flow, the sports person is more likely to perform well, as their focus is intensely on the execution of skills. Attention is focused on the skills or on the input from the senses relevant to the sport. It is in flow that you are not even aware of yourself, have complete neutrality over the quality of the execution of your skills during the performance and are unaware of the spectators, judges and expectations of others. In other words, you are completely in control of your actions and reactions and are in an altered state of conscious alertness which feels powerful. Achieving flow can be easier than it sounds. Thinking and perceiving that your skills are good enough to meet the needs of the contest is important, as is not becoming bored by the competition itself. But, above all, being relaxed, focused and thinking positively, eliminating all negative thoughts, will develop your ability to flow. Make sure you don't force yourself to flow, as it needs to develop naturally, and practise training your attention so that you have distraction under control.

Look good, feel confident

It may sound shallow, but what you wear when playing sports can have a direct impact on your results. Of course, it's important to feel comfortable, but it is also well recognised by the sports professionals I have worked with that wearing something that psychologically triggers confidence can increase and maintain high levels of performance in the chosen game or sport. You are well advised to wear something that not only looks good, but mentally reminds you of a previous win, as this will unconsciously trigger confidence. Conversely, wearing something that feels uncomfortable and has no relation to feeling confident in the past is going to add little to your performance, and indeed may even be a block to you achieving the best result possible.

Stretch yourself

There is only a single direction in sport, and that is forwards not backwards. Setting small achievable goals to step up your game is important if you want to move from division two to division one. Remember that doing what you have always done will only achieve what you have always got, so it really is important to think about cranking up the amount you stretch yourself. Stretching yourself isn't just about your actual performance, but may include performing in front of a larger audience or doing a live media interview for the first time.

Stretching yourself will give you the 'ouch' factor, but remember – no pain, no gain.

Copy the best

There can be no doubt that all sports enthusiasts observe the performances of their idols. I recall working with an ice-dance couple who explained that they would spend hours watching footage of Jayne Torvill and Christopher Dean to identify and mentally process their pure excellence in the sport. The same can be said of my nephew, who spends hours looking at Wayne Rooney and how he plays his game. My nephew then goes down to the local park, always attempting to mimic Rooney's excellence. The copycat tool described in chapter 7 helps not only to improve skills, but will do wonders for your confidence during the game or competition. When sports people perform at the top of their game, they will have copied many of the attitudes, traits and techniques that masters of their sport have used before them. What often happens is that they copy the skills and then use their confidence to develop their own styles and techniques to make themselves even better.

Be confident in sport: the script

The following script is designed to embed positive suggestions into your mind, so that you increase your confidence in sport. To use the script, sit comfortably in a quiet, warm room, place your hands on your thighs, relax deeply by letting all your muscles become heavy and tired and then count down slowly from ten to one. Once you are relaxed, slowly read the script to yourself. Alternatively, you may get someone to read the script to you slowly, as you relax comfortably with your eyes closed. If you choose to do this, it is best to signal that you are ready to begin by lifting one of your index fingers rather than speaking out loud, so that your relaxation isn't disturbed. Notice that there are intervals between certain words to help ensure the script sinks deep into your mind.

And I would like you to remain feeling calm and at ease ... aware of the sounds around ... you ... reassuring you that you are completely safe and secure ... these sounds form a backdrop to my voice ... my voice ... which you follow ... my voice is a guide ... and ... you have nothing to do ... nothing to concern yourself with ... in fact ... all you have to do is listen to my voice ... as you sit there with increasing ease ... I would like to take you on a guided tour ...

What you can know ... is that all I say to you ... will, exactly as I say it, increase your confidence ... your self-esteem ... your performance in your sport ... as we set off on this confident journey ... to a place of calm ... a tranquil and refreshing place ... your place ... your place of confidence ... a place where you build your confidence in your sport ... and you can even be aware of the fragrance of the air as you come on this journey ... you are now aware of the sense of ease that you are feeling ... feeling warm and comfortable ...

That sense of feeling so at ease and comfortable ... a sense of being so secure in yourself ... you may even experience a warm glow spreading through your whole body ... and you can allow that glow to spread even deeper ... and deeper into your being ... because you deserve it ... as we continue ... on this wonderful journey to confidence ... confidence in your game ... confidence in your abilities ... confidence in your sports results ... you may become aware of the sounds around you ... maybe sounds of the birds singing ... or sounds of calm ...

You may even see the colours changing on this journey to confidence...as we move on...and shortly...just beyond...we will arrive at our destination...ahead you will see a golden tub...a bit like a wishing well...a well of well-being and confidence...and as you now look at the tub...you see it has your name on it...and perhaps you can even see an image on it...an image of you...a still picture of you playing your sport...begin now to make your way to this golden tub...and as you look closely, there is a cup hanging...a golden cup...with your name inscribed on it...

As you look at the golden tub...you now see a sign which reads 'menu'...see the words...on the menu, which you can just make out...there are various words...self-esteem...fulfilment...relaxation...confidence...strength...courage...focus...strong muscles...health...laughter...and there may be even more you can see...and when you are ready you can dip your golden cup into the golden tub and have as much of these as you want...as these all help increase your sports performance...and your confidence to enjoy your sport...

And all these options on the menu are completely free...they feed your mind...and maintain a lean, fit...and now...when you are full...you can enjoy digesting all you chose from the menu...as your choice from the menu sinks deeper and deeper into your mind...and your choice from the menu...now sinks deeper still into your unconscious mind...and when you are ready to return to this room...feeling mentally well fed...fed full of confidence in your sport...feeling secure in your confidence and self-worth...you can gently begin to open your eyes with new learnings...safe and secure back here in the room...

Real Life

Lizzy

Lizzy, 17, a professional gymnast, visited me to help increase her confidence in front of a crowd.

She explained that every time she was called to perform, she would lose focus and confidence in front of the crowd. She was incredibly gifted as a gymnast, but the more she was aware that her confidence took a knock as soon as she heard the roar of the crowd, the more anxious she became. I worked with Lizzy over three weeks, the objective being to help her calm down and gain focus as soon as she was called to perform, whether it was in a closed training session or in front of the public and press at a major competition.

At the first session, I decided to teach Lizzy progressive relaxation and coached her how to use this an hour before she was due to take to the mat. Between week one and week two, Lizzy was asked to email me with her progress daily.

In week two, I decided to conduct a session of clinical hypnotherapy and utilised the soap opera technique. Lizzy found this form of guided imagery very useful, as she was able to associate herself with the image; in other words, she was able to mentally get into the zone. In between weeks two and three, Lizzy was asked to practise the guided-imagery soap opera technique, which she did successfully, until she was comfortable imagining that she was performing really well in front of an appreciative crowd.

Finally, in week three, I coached Lizzy in how to acquire 'flow' in her performance. I decided to do this at her local sports arena and set up a small audience to test her ability to gain full focus on the execution of her performance. As Lizzy had previously practised relaxation and the soap opera technique, she was set up to flow well. I was delighted to hear from Lizzy several months later, when she told me that she had won a number of medals nationally.

Carlos

Carlos, who at 22 years of age was a professional goalkeeper, contacted me to help build his confidence and performance after his team lost a run of crucial games. Playing for a top team and not achieving the wins that they needed had left Carlos with a thought process bathed in self—put-downs. They were obviously focused on the times when he'd failed to keep goals out during the last six games for his club.

During session one, it was important to coach Carlos to let go of the past and we agreed that we would spend one hour maximum talking about the past, then draw a line and move forward in a positive frame of mind. Having allowed Carlos to revel in self-pity for an hour, I very assertively made it clear to him that he would now move forward and build his self-confidence back up. He agreed to monitor his self-talk and begin affirming himself more positively, using more appropriate language patterns.

In session two, I conducted clinical hypnotherapy designed to help Carlos let go of any remaining self-doubt, before using guided imagery to programme his unconscious mind to regain focus on his game. I also coached Carlos to use self-hypnosis and the flow technique, which he found particularly useful, as tools to prepare himself for his next match. Between sessions two and three, Carlos agreed to develop the flow technique in practice games, which he managed to do really well, in addition to continuing to carry out his self-hypnosis.

In our final session, I decided to conduct a hypnotherapy session and utilise the soap opera technique to further programme his mind to focus and use the skills needed to help win the next game.

Carlos went on to put in a series of performances for his team that not only helped them to claw back a string of winning matches, but also get promoted for the next season. Carlos is now one of the UK's top goalies and tells me that he continues to use the techniques to programme what he calls 'a confident and winning mind'.

Jess

Inspired by the repeated success stories of the UK's men's and women's cycling teams, Jess had ambitions of being one of the country's top cyclists and going to the next Olympic games. She was performing at the top of her game and winning competition after competition. Her problem came when she was out on a training ride and was knocked off her bike in a road accident and badly injured. She got over the physical injuries pretty quickly, but her confidence to ride at full speed had really suffered. After hearing about the work I had done with a number of leading sports people, Jess came to me to ask for support in building back her self-confidence so that she could ride with the best of them again.

We quickly established that whenever she dug deep to go at full tilt on her bike, she would see images in her mind of her road accident and the pain of recovering. It was a tough one to crack, but I had to work hard on

Jess to help her put the past into the past and to keep it from coming back and dashing her confidence all over again. We agreed that she had permission to let go of the memories that were dragging her back and also that it was okay to get angry and, in fact, that she could focus the anger into adding extra speed during her training and competitions.

I also helped Jess to focus her mind and imagination on dealing with the unexpected, which can happen in cycling, especially when it comes to other competitors in races and road users in training. She was able to start to work on improving her skills in anticipating the unexpected and this added heaps to her self-confidence.

What happened to Jess was outstanding. Within four weeks, she was out on the roads and beating her own distance and time challenges by miles. Her training has come on in leaps and bounds and she's building up to the Olympic trial standard time with a series of competitions.

7 Secrets of Confidence

Your secrets

- Don't hold on to past 'failures'.

- Set realistic goals and be excited about them.

- Practise relaxation techniques to help you chill out.

- Practise guided imagery daily to program your unconscious mind.

- Learn to 'flow' to help improve your focused concentration.

- Step out of your comfort zone to increase your performance.

- Copy the best in the game.

Confident About the Future

17

This is something that continues to play on the minds of millions of people. Building a bright and confident future for ourselves and others can be within the grasp of us all if we are open and willing to put in the work. A bright future will, of course, mean different things to different people, depending on their personal values. In this chapter, I set out the practical strategies to help create a future in which you can be proud, excited and, most of all, confident. But do remember that this confident future is unlikely to be something that happens to you by accident or good fortune; you will most definitely need to put in the effort.

> **Building a bright and confident future for ourselves and others can be within the grasp of us all**

Picture the future as current reality

We are all blessed with magical imaginations, but sadly we limit ourselves when it comes to using them as we get older. The dreams seem to fade as we age, limited by our own 'what ifs' and 'yes buts'. It is as though a 'no entry' sign halts our ability to see what really can be when it comes to success, wealth, happiness and confidence. Let go of this blockage, I say, and begin to dream of what your confident future looks like, sounds like and feels like as current reality. Rather than saying to yourself, 'I will be . . .' say 'I am . . .' In your mind, associate yourself with the confident future, as opposed to seeing it in the distance and remaining detached. And be sure to accept that you deserve a confident future. If doubts creep in, see that bright-red stop sign, smile and affirm that you do deserve a confident future. Reflect on your confident future every day as a current reality, so that you get into the confident zone. One key tip is to go out and buy a quality notebook, one that you think looks and feels really good, and write down how your confident future looks, sounds and feels every day. But remember to write it in the present tense, affirming that the confident future is here NOW!

Believe in the belief

As you zone into what your confident future looks, sounds and feels like, it is important to allow yourself to believe in the belief that you deserve it and that it really is *your* future. You must let go of the 'oh, it will never happen to me' philosophy. Set yourself up for a realistic, confident future, but do not limit yourself! As someone who was jobless, depressed and taking medication for panic attacks, it would have been so easy for me to self-limit and create a dead-end future. I chose the other route, painted out a confident future, zoned in on this as though it was already here and shouted, 'Bollocks!' if I ever doubted or failed to believe in myself and my future. You too can do the same. Believing in the belief means that every day you must recognise that this confident future is yours, you deserve it, you believe it and you are excited by it.

Do it, as well as thinking it

I emphasise that I am a realist in all my books. To suggest for one minute that belief is the only thing that matters in order to create a confident future will not achieve what you want – you have to 'walk the talk' as well.

Over the years, I have encountered hundreds of self-styled philosophical gurus who rave on about manifesting a rosy future through thought alone. Don't get me wrong, that does have a part to play, but do you honestly think sitting cross-legged meditating in a quiet room, day after day, expecting great things to simply happen will actually turn them into a reality? I think not. To this end, it is important that you are proactive and make your confident future actually happen for real. List down all the things that you need to do and then prioritise them. Then it's JFDI. Get out there and make it happen.

Be envious rather than jealous

Jealousy, unlike envy, is a vicious, negative emotion that only damages one person – you. It creates anger, vengefulness and eats away at your own self-worth and personal growth. Envy, on the other hand, is about longing for something someone else has without the calculated vindictiveness that jealousy stirs. Envy is, in fact, healthy, if it is channelled appropriately, as it can trigger motivation and prepare you to take action so you get your slice of the cake. Years ago, I would look at my own personal coach with sheer envy. I wanted what she had. I respected her style, her skills, her ability, her presence. But I didn't feel vindictive, wanting her to fail; quite the contrary. I loved my sessions with her and became really ambitious to achieve what she had managed to do so well. With self-belief and hard work, I did just that and still thank her for feeding me well with plenty of things that I wanted to aspire to. As you look at those who have what you want, be envious rather than jealous. Become jealous and you may just find your future is crushed, as you think there's no way you will get what the other person has and simply do nothing positive to move yourself forward to their position.

Stay resilient

As Billy Ocean sings, 'When the going gets tough, the tough get going!' As you build your confident future, don't expect it to be all plain sailing to a land of milk and honey. We all have ups and downs and it really is important to stay resilient and never give up. There are a number of actions to take if you sense you are wobbling:

1 Increase exercise. Get your heart pumping and allow an increase in exercise to make positive changes within your body and mind. The endorphin-release triggered by exercise is the only drug you will need. There is always something you can do, such as running, walking, biking, hiking, swimming or playing sports.

2 Have a belly laugh. When times are a bit tough, it's useful to find your sense of humour. Try visiting a comedy club, watching a funny film, meeting up with a friend who makes you laugh or, if it takes your fancy, tickling yourself! This will help not only with your emotional state, but also your physical well-being.

3 Keep visualising. Make sure you keep practising your visualisation, seeing, hearing and feeling what you want for your future.

4 Exercise your brain. Mentally strong or emotionally resilient people ensure that they use their brains. It is, after all an organ, so it must be used. Playing brain games can be really useful. Try out right-brain/left-brain exercises such as puzzles and card and memory games; brush your teeth with the opposite hand; find a new way to get home after work.

5 Relax. Practise some of the chill tips outlined in chapter 3. This will ensure you stay cool and avoid letting your emotions run all over you.

Hang out with the radiators

As you move on to develop a successful and confident future, the last thing you want is to be surrounded by a bunch of losers whose only pleasure in life is entering the 'victim of the year' competition. Think for a moment about your circle of friends. Do they offer you something? Do they inspire you? Do they enthuse about your dreams? Do they join in the celebrations when you achieve something big? Do they give you as much time as you give them? Think of each friend individually. If the answer is yes, hold on to. If, on the other hand, it is a definite no, bin them. Stop taking their calls and when they have a tantrum because you haven't been listening to all that's happening in their lives, simply ignore them. This also applies to partners. If all they do is moan, groan and pull you down, bin them. They offer you nothing and are, quite frankly, a drain on your life. You deserve better.

Learn something new every day

It takes an arrogant person to say they have nothing left to learn in life – and a naive one at that. Successful people who are confident about their future make it their mission to learn. They appreciate that knowledge and experience is the food that helps them to grow. They are alert, they listen and they are hungry to seek out new experiences. Your confident future will be based on your knowledge and your skills, so it is important that you open your mind and your heart to learning something new every single day.

> " Successful people who are confident about their future make it their mission to learn "

Never be afraid to ask if you can experience something so that you learn. We are conditioned not to ask for what we need, but I want to encourage you to be a little cheeky and ask those who can provide you with an opportunity to learn. Those people you ask will often feel pleased that you have asked them, even honoured, so don't be shy. Ask and eventually you will receive. If a confident future means attaining a qualification, go out there and sort it. Don't wait for tomorrow; do it today. Action, action, action!

Be confident about your future

The following script is designed to embed positive sugges-tions into your mind, so that you increase your confidence to bring in a confident future. To use the script, sit comfortably in a quiet, warm room, place your hands on your thighs, relax deeply by letting all your muscles become heavy and tired and then count down slowly from ten to one. Once you are relaxed, slowly read the script to yourself. Alternatively, get someone to read the script to you slowly, as you relax comfortably with your eyes closed. If you choose to do this, it is best to signal that you are ready to begin by lifting one of your index fingers rather than speaking out loud, so that your relaxation isn't disturbed. Notice that there are intervals between certain words to help ensure the script sinks deep into your mind.

As you relax ... I want you to know that your mind ... understands that you are becoming more and more focused ... more focused than you have been in a long ... long time ... and you can become even more relaxed ... twice as relaxed ... go as deep into that wonderful state of physical and mental relaxation as you wish ... and as you relax even more ... your unconscious mind ... is alert ... is ready to accept these things ... all for your benefit ...

And should you wish ... you can experience a more deeply relaxed state than you have felt in a long time ... because you enjoy these feelings of ease ... as you let go ... let go of any unnecessary nervous tension ... and all that is important is that you enjoy drifting ... a bit like a beautiful daydream ... and this dream that I now take you on ... will happen exactly as I say it will happen ... all for your benefit ... all for you ... this dream will sink deeper into your unconscious mind ... and your unconscious mind understands that it is for your benefit . . .

And now . . . as you drift . . . I want you to bring into your mind . . . your confident future . . . whatever that may look like . . . sound like . . . feel like . . . smell like . . . even taste like . . . I want you to enjoy the dream of that confident future . . . and really associate yourself with the dream . . . enter into it . . . be it . . . live it and allow it to sink deep into your mind . . . imagine it moving into the centre of your mind . . . and as it does so, I want you to turn up the brightness . . . the sound and the excited feelings . . .

With your eyes closed . . . I now want you to allow your mind to go blank for a moment . . . and I want you now to imagine all of the things you did to make this confident future become a living reality . . . focus on what you did . . . how you did it . . . think of the activities you did to make sure your confident future turned from dream to reality . . . and for the next minute or so . . . pay attention to them one by one . . . as you do so . . . I want you to know that these activities sink into your unconscious processes . . . embedded deep . . . like success habits, so to speak . . .

These success habits . . . are now firmly a part of you, both inside and outside of this room . . . you will now be reminded of these habits . . . so that you feel motivated . . . driven . . . enthused . . . excited . . . to carry them out . . . action them . . . action them daily . . . weekly and monthly as needed . . . all for your benefit . . . and because you enjoy taking action you are so solidly conditioned to build your confident future . . . you can be pleased . . . sure in the knowledge that your future is confident . . . your mind is now programmed so that you build the confident future you want to build for yourself . . .

Real Life

Berkeley

I met Berkeley in mid 2009, when he was 28 years old, and found his story inspiring. He told me how he had set up his confident future. He explained that in 1999 he had a record deal with a major label, but at that time hadn't quite developed enough as a songwriter and needed a lot of help. He also didn't really know his mind back then, so all the decisions that had to be made regarding his future were made by other people. The record deal eventually fell apart and Berkeley felt crushed because he didn't know how to make things happen for himself or, more to the point, that he could make things happen for himself.

The situation got worse when he became the victim of terrible medical misdiagnosis. Berkeley lost the full use of his hands for four years, which he was told was caused by arthritis, and had a lingering case of Bell's Palsy. It was during this period of illness that he decided to build a confident future for himself. He felt useless and had to work out a way to make a life for himself if the use of his hands didn't come back. He started to really think about what he wanted from life and how he could achieve it in his situation.

Even though he had lost a lot of his very basic physical powers, he knew that his way forward was to accept his situation and take control of his life and his choices. By taking control of his future, Berkeley would feel good about himself, more confident and optimistic that things would happen. He explained to me that in building his confident future, he never wallowed in self-pity. Instead, he took action and eventually found out that he had been misdiagnosed and had a severe case of carpal tunnel syndrome caused by a vitamin B deficiency. Feeling confident about his health made him equally confident about his future and he explained that he could see, hear and feel himself working full time again.

With passion and determination, Berkeley got a job as a theatre director and before long the Bell's palsy had cleared up. Taking action, he began to act again, something he had done years before. Berkeley was headstrong and determined to act again, as he knew that acting was something that would lift his confidence — and it did just that. He was cast as Laertes in a touring production of Hamlet and was subsequently cast in eight other touring productions in a three-year period.

Further building his confident future, Berkeley continues to work on his songs and sees his future clear in his mind. He speaks enthusiastically about his catalogue of songs and a solo project that he is working on. It is evident that he believes in the belief that he will be successful and experience has taught him how to stay resilient. He is about to promote his projects to record companies and managers and this time recognises that he is in charge of his music projects and will make decisions for himself. But it doesn't end there. Berkeley is about to meet with a top literary agent to help secure his debut publishing deal as a children's novelist. Berkeley is a shining example of someone who had incredible emotional resilience and who went on to power up his self-belief. And he actually went out and did it, rather than just talk about it.

Caroline

I first met Caroline in 2007. At that time she was a 34-year-old marketing manager and was divorced with two children. She wanted to create a future for herself that would be financially secure and perhaps later meet Mr Right.

Working with Caroline, I first of all spent time defining the vision of what a confident future really looked like. The future had to excite her and drive her passions and she really needed to acknowledge that she deserved it, having had a messy break-up with her ex-partner.

Caroline told me she could see herself as a marketing director with a fast-paced retail business, earning an £80K salary, driving an Audi sports car, wearing designer suits and dating 'a top-of-the-range geezer', as she so wonderfully put it! Having set the vision, we cleared up issues from the past and agreed there would be no future discussion about 'Mr Toss Pot', her ex-husband — he was discarded to the dustbin of the past. Instead, it was time for action and to make the vision become reality.

In session two, we identified all the practical actions Caroline was to do to make the confident future come alive. I then conducted a motivational hypnotherapy session, embedding the vision of the confident future and the consistent actions Caroline was going to do. It was important to also show Caroline that I totally believed in her and to send her out of my consulting room totally excited, motivated and self-believing. She also agreed that she would carry out the first few immediate actions, which were to apply for a couple of marketing director positions she had seen advertised and practise self-hypnosis, which I had taught her in session one.

In session three, our final session, I delivered a straight-talking motivational coaching session to support Caroline as she moved forward. During this session, she agreed to ditch any drains in her life, of which there were a few, and to only hang out with the radiators. Following on from this, I went through a hypnotherapy session with her designed to seal the confident future in Caroline's mind and ensure the success habits to support this were in place.

Six months later, Caroline was appointed marketing director for a large fashion business and has recently begun dating the man of her dreams and enjoys posing in her soft-top Audi.

Lucy

Lucy made an appointment to see me because she didn't have the confidence in herself to make the decision to accept or turn down a life-changing job offer. She was a young fashion designer, aged just 24. Following a bit of work experience with a design house in the UK, she'd been head-hunted to head up a small team at a New York fashion house. You may think that this was a no-brainer. Well, remember that we are all very different people and Lucy had her reasons for being doubtful.

When we met, she told me that the real issue was a complete lack of confidence in her own abilities and she was scared of making a fool of herself, being tasked with managing a small team of people. She had to shine, both in terms of her creative flair and also her ability to manage other people.

I told Lucy to practise imagining what it would be like to actually be in New York and working with her colleagues to fulfil a client brief, to picture herself confidently being in control of the situation and tasking her colleagues with what they needed to do to make sure that deadlines and expectations were fulfilled. To back up the mind games I tasked her with, I also helped Lucy to quickly pick up some management tasks and get a little experience of taking responsibility. She did this in two ways: by confidently asking her present employer if she could lead a project and also by reading up on a little management theory.

A year later, Lucy bit the bullet and flew out to New York to take her career up to the next level in the world of fashion design. She sent me an arty postcard of the Statue of Liberty, proclaiming that she was literally on top of the world and thanking me for my support and guidance.

7 Secrets of Confidence

Your secrets

- The future is now. Start to picture how you want it to be.

- You deserve the future you want.

- Start to take actions to shape your future.

- Learn to take some rough with the smooth.

- Surround yourself with radiators who have a positive influence on you.

- Be confident about your future.

Part 3

Off You Go!

Be Confident in Three Weeks

Having worked as a confidence expert for the last ten years, I know that it is absolutely possible for the majority of people to increase their confidence to a decent level in three weeks. Here, I'm going to outline how you can, with a little effort, increase your confidence in three weeks. Three weeks, or 21 days, works because research has shown that it takes our minds that amount of time to enforce a good habit. In other words, do something to support your confidence for 21 days and you will certainly experience a positive shift upwards in your confidence and self-esteem. The programme that I outline is based on my 7 Secrets. If you are suffering from clinical depression or epilepsy, seek medical advice from your GP before undertaking the following protocol.

> ❝ Here, I'm going to outline how you can, with a little effort, increase your confidence in three weeks ❞

Week One

Monday

- Write down all of the negative issues from the past that are holding you back. Don't hold back; make sure you note everything, even if you think it's not that significant.

- As you look at them, agree from within that you are willing to release them. If this triggers emotions, let it all out when you are ready to do so, in a safe and comfortable environment.

- When you have released your emotions, smile as you tear up the list of issues and put it in the bin. Smile again and tell yourself that this is the first day of the rest of your life.

Tuesday

- Go for a long, relaxing walk and keep telling yourself that you deserve to be confident and it is now your time.

- When you return from the walk, write down all of the thoughts you have about yourself (if any) that relate to having to be perfect. For example: 'I have to get everything right first time' or 'I must be perfect or I will lose my job' or 'I have to look my best or no one will want to know me.' I only want you to spend ten minutes on this process. Look at what you have written, laugh out loud and yell, 'What utter crap!'

- Acknowledge this and tell yourself that you are fallible and being perfect is bad for the health. Acknowledge that from now on you will accept that you do not have to be perfect.

Wednesday

- Do something today that makes you feel really good about yourself. For example, treat yourself to a new outfit, buy tickets for a concert or book a weekend break.

- Walk tall today and tell yourself that you are a real winner. Think 'confidence' and deliberately pay attention to the confident body language that matches your thoughts.

- Write down what it feels like to be confident. Increase the intensity of the feelings as you write.

Thursday

- Practise relaxation as set out in chapter 3. Don't worry if you find it a little difficult at first. Practice really does make perfect.

- Practise these relaxation techniques three times during the day and enjoy them.

- As you relax, be aware how much it helps you focus your concentration.

Friday

- In relaxation, play some of the mind games described in chapter 4. Test out a few and find the one that works the best for you.

- Practise playing your favourite mind game several times.

- Finally, write down six positive things that you got from playing your favourite mind game.

Saturday

- Once again play your mind game, but this time it is important to consciously smile as you do so.

- During the day act 'as if' you are confident, paying attention to how you walk, talk and interact with others. Imagine you are confident all day, and be it.

- Treat yourself in the evening to reward your efforts. Perhaps watch your favourite film, have a glass of champagne to toast your success or have an early night with someone rather tasty!

Week Two

Sunday

- Identify what aspects of your personal image you want to improve most and list them down. This may include your hair, clothes, nails, skin, weight and so on.

- Look at the list and identify the main priority. If improving the priority is going to make you feel much better about yourself, it is time for action.

- Dip into chapter 5 for ideas to help take the appropriate action.

Monday

- Carry out the action you identified yesterday. This may include booking an appointment at a top salon or arranging for a personal stylist to help improve your wardrobe.

- If there are other actions you need to take to brand yourself brilliant, list them down and next to each put a date by when you will have executed the action.

- Do some deep relaxation and practise your mind game.

Tuesday

- Begin thinking about tasks you could make yourself do over the next couple of days that will stretch your confidence. Now write them down.

- Choose three of them and begin, in relaxation, to see, hear and feel yourself carrying them out.

- Select one that you can do tomorrow.

Wednesday

- Use the soap opera technique described on page 71 to mentally rehearse the task you will do today to stretch your confidence.

- Go out and do the task that stretches your confidence.

- Celebrate the completion of the task and prepare to do the other two tasks tomorrow.

Thursday

- Go out and do the other two tasks that will stretch your confidence.

- Treat yourself to something special as a reward for completing these tasks and recognise how successful you have been and affirm to yourself that you are capable of doing many things.

- Carry out one of the mind games described in chapter 4.

Friday

- Do something today that makes you feel great about your image. For example, go out and buy something new to wear or arrange a facial; anything that is good for your image and makes you feel on top of the world.

- Practise relaxation and use the command and deliver technique described on page 68 to boost your confidence.

- Do some moderate exercise, such as going for a walk or playing a sport that makes you feel good.

Saturday

- Go out and do a task that helps stretch your confidence. Again, remind yourself just how good it feels to be growing in confidence.

- Write down how good it feels to be confident and describe in detail what you are now doing differently as a confident person. Be sure to write this in the present tense.

- Do something that makes you laugh today. Perhaps watch a funny film or go to a comedy club.

Week Three

Sunday

- Take time for yourself today. Do exactly what you want to do.

- During the day, keep seeing yourself full of confidence and notice how good it feels to be confident.

- Deliberately act as if you are confident all day, paying attention to your body language and the way you communicate with those around you.

Monday

- As you go about your business, deliberately observe people who project confidence.

- Notice what they do, how they walk, talk, move and engage with other people.

7 Secrets of Confidence

- As you observe confident people, think about what you can take from it, what you can copy.

Tuesday

- Think again about the people you observed yesterday and what they did to be confident.

- In relaxation, see, hear and feel yourself doing exactly what they did.

- Deliberately go out of your way to mimic what those confident people did.

Wednesday

- Think about all the people you spend time with and identify who are the emotional drains and who are the radiators. Make the conscious decision to ditch those drains and nurture your relationships with the radiators.

- Identify something that you would like to do that you have never had the confidence to do, something that will make you happy. Take action to make it happen.

- In relaxation, imagine the feeling of confidence filling every fibre of your body. Intensify the feelings and smile, knowing that confidence is now a firm part of your being.

Thursday

- Select a piece of music that makes you feel confident. Remind yourself that every time you want to immediately boost your confidence, you will hear this music in your mind.

- Do something that stretches your confidence and recognise just how confident you feel now you are able to do the things that you never thought would be possible.

- Mingle with strangers and act as if you are totally confident.

Friday

- Spend time with a friend today, one who makes you feel really good about yourself.

- Deliberately dress to impress today. Let it remind you that looking good makes you feel good, and that in turn makes you feel confident.

- Mentally repeat over and over to yourself just how good it feels to be so confident. Walk and talk confidently all day, and enjoy it!

Saturday

- Select a mind game from chapter 4 and practise it.

- Remind yourself that you have moved on so much and that your confidence will increase daily.

- Observe someone who is, in your eyes, confident. Identify what you can copy from them.

Sunday

- Revel in a personal celebration today! Treat yourself lots.

- Remind yourself just how good it feels to have adopted the 7 Secrets of Confidence.

- Email me at info@stevemillertraining.com and tell me all about your success.

Real Life

Katie

Katie, aged 38, had a crisis of confidence during a fraught adoption process that she and her husband had been going through for over two years.

With tears in her eyes, she told me that she'd spent years trying to fall pregnant, but after going down all the routes available, she'd agreed with her husband that all that was left for them was adoption. Adopting a child is a tough process and I know they want people who are completely sure they can handle the practical and emotional demands of raising a child, but Katie had lost her self-confidence just two months before a final interview panel with the professionals who would grant them the right to adopt.

For her, the pressure had become too much and she now couldn't see how she could be herself and clearly and confidently explain why and how they were the best family for this child.

I knew this was what she had given her heart and soul to, and we agreed to go through the 21 day confidence programme that is set out above. I made it clear to Katie that she had to stick to the programme and asked her to give me feedback every day and to go over with me any particular concerns that she had.

A week after completing the programme, Katie came back to see me to discuss where she was in terms of getting back her confidence to go for the child that she and her husband dreamt of. The change was there for anyone to see — she held her head high, looked me in the eye, smiled and said, 'We are going to have our son in two months' time and I can't wait.' The fear and trepidation had been blown far away and she was set to meet the adoption panel.

I can tell you that two years down the line, Katie, her husband and their son Carl are a complete, tight and confident family unit.

How to Maintain Your Confidence

Building confidence is one thing; maintaining it is another. Humans are fallible, so of course there will be periods in your life when your confidence takes a dip. In this chapter, I have brought together ten confidence-maintaining tips that will help ensure your confidence remains healthy. They will repair your confidence any time it takes a knock and no one will know that you have one or two chinks in your armour.

1   **Don't keep comparing yourself to other people**
    Make sure you avoid the urge to consistently compare yourself to other people. If you continue to compare yourself to others and value yourself negatively, you will simply destroy the esteem you have built. Of course, learning from others is fine and healthy envy can motivate, but drowning yourself in negative comparisons will burst your confidence bubble.

2   Find some new radiators

If you have a shortage of enthusiastic and inspirational friends, go out and find some. You will be infected by their positive attitude, as opposed to being drained by the negative victims whom I hope you have already binned from your life.

" They will repair your confidence any time it takes a knock "

3   Do things you love

If you are in a job you hate, look around for a new one. It is important to make changes in your life, so that you are involved and engaged in work and other activities that truly make you happy and valued. Of course, this can take time, but by taking action, you will automatically begin to protect your confidence. The same goes for hobbies and interests; do what you are passionate about and it will be like taking a feel-good drug.

4   Stamp on your critic

If you notice that you begin to put yourself down frequently, quickly take control of it by seeing a bright-red stop sign. It can be so easy to allow that little demon voice in your head to poison your mind with put-downs, so stamp on it quickly. Instead, continue to mentally talk positively about yourself and remind yourself that negative thoughts are weak and positive thoughts are strong.

5   Be yourself

Rather than letting others control your life, just be yourself. Don't let others control your life; if they try, bin them from your life, as they are simply self-centred bullies. Allowing someone else to control your life will only mean you lose your self-respect and never feel good about yourself. If you find yourself making decisions based on getting approval from other people, it means you aren't being true to yourself and your confidence will falter. So make sure you continue to value yourself, your opinions and your right to live the life you want. Remember, you weren't born to please other people.

6   List down your achievements

Frequently make a list of the things you have done that you once thought were impossible. This will help trigger a sense of pride, so it's important to read the list frequently. You can even go a step further and relive those break-throughs by closing your eyes and imagining them again. And as well as listing your achievements, write down your personal qualities, to remind yourself what a talented individual you are. This will help you focus on your strengths rather than your weaknesses and help you see yourself in a positive light for the long haul.

7   Forget analysing yourself

Too much self-analysis can sometimes turn into nasty bacteria, and that's the trouble with a lot of traditional therapy, which focuses on analysing you. It does little to move people on and keeps them static. We can, at times, overanalyse ourselves, which does nothing for our self-esteem. If you find yourself doing this too much, give it a rest.

8   Give yourself a clap

Make sure you congratulate yourself frequently, and enjoy it. When you achieve something, don't simply move on to the next task in hand, but instead give yourself a clap and accept that you have done well. The same goes when others pay you compliments. Don't dismiss them, accept them by simply saying 'thank you'.

9   Get lots of exercise

I am a big fan of exercise, but this doesn't mean you have to join the gym. Exercise will decrease stress hormones and increase endorphins, which make you feel fabulous. Try different types of exercise so you don't get bored and if exercise is new to you, simply start by going for a good walk in the fresh air. Not only will the exercise make you feel good, but it will also help you to look better as you lose any excess weight you may have. Also remember that exercise has lots of other spin-off benefits, especially when it comes to improving your mental attitude. One thing I take from exercise is that it helps me to take my mind off problems and see things in a better light.

10 Actions speak louder than words

Sitting around moaning that your confidence has taken a knock will achieve nothing. It is crucial you take action to feel better and increase your self-confidence. Doing nothing will only feed stress, anxiety and depression, so make sure you do something proactive to help yourself. Remember, it is your responsibility and not anyone else's.

Confidence: the keeping-it-real *check list*

- Do you feel calm in unfamiliar surroundings and situations?

- Are you able to talk to anyone and everyone?

- Have you moved on from being your number one critic to accepting you're not perfect?

- Are you satisfied with your mind and body?

- Can you live for tomorrow as well as today and smile?

- List what you want to achieve from your life in the next 6, 12 and 24 months

---

Real Life

Pete

Pete was a successful manager when he came to see me a year ago. At the age of 44, he felt, with some justification, that he was ready to step up to the top tier of management and join the board of the company that he'd worked at for over 11 years. A spot had come up to be the next operations director and he'd been the number two in the operations section.

To cut a long story short, Pete put his hat into the ring for the board-level promotion, only to find that an external candidate had beaten him to it. As you can imagine, he was gutted to have been overlooked for the top spot and was nursing a badly dented confidence.

Helping Pete was pretty simple, and it started with accepting that he was his own harshest critic and that the overanalysing of his actions and what could have been was holding him back. I told him to note down all the positive things that he'd achieved for his employer and to start thinking of moving on to pastures green, where someone with his considerable experience and skills could take a top role.

I also asked Pete to look at what he loved in life and what could give him the extra confidence and drive to reach out for a new job and possibly a new life. It turned out that he was passionate about military aircraft and that's where every spare moment he had was directed. I asked him if he'd ever considered putting his operations and logistics experience and qualifications to the test with an organisation involved in the history of military planes. 'No,' he said, 'what a wonderful idea?' He then went away, beaming, promising to research the museums and restoration societies that dot the country and to get in touch with them.

After firing his CV off to a couple of dozen potentials, he was rewarded with an interview at a major air museum near London that needed someone to help plan the acquisition and transportation of new and existing exhibits. After a little more confidence-boosting aimed at firing his interview skills, I can tell you that Pete now heads up a large team who spend their waking hours moving aircraft from place to place and probably dream about their jobs at night as well.

Working With a Confidence Coach

20

This isn't for everybody, but sometimes it can be useful to source an expert who is appropriately trained and experienced in helping others to rapidly increase their self-confidence.

Be aware that some confidence coaches will be much better than others and that they will obviously charge you money for their services. You only have to surf the net these days to find thousands of individuals claiming to be experts in improving people's confidence. Deciding who to work with can often be the tricky part, so it's important to do your homework and not jump in head first and choose the first one that you like the look of. There are six key checks you should make before spending your money, and it is only once these are satisfied that you should book your first consultation.

> Be aware that some confidence coaches will be much better than others

Check 1: What qualifies them?

It is possible for anyone in the UK to brand themselves as a confidence coach. The market isn't regulated, so beware that you may be contacting someone who has no qualifications and little or no professional experience. Start by finding out where they trained and if they belong to a professional body. If they claim to have a professional qualification, ask who it is accredited by. If it was attained by distance learning, you are best advised to move on and call someone else, in my opinion. After all, would you be motivated to be a passenger in a car driven by someone who learnt to drive by distance learning? Once you have checked on qualifications, ask them if they specialise in confidence. If the answer is no, again move on. If they claim to be a confidence specialist, ask them what specific areas within confidence they specialise in. Ask them how long they have been working as a confidence coach and if the answer is less than two years, think twice before booking an appointment.

Check 2: Do you have confidence in them?

When you make your enquiry, assess how confident they sound in themselves. If you have a hunch that they aren't very confident, look elsewhere. Also, think about how inspired you were by the person at the end of the phone. Did you feel enthused to work with them, excited, and did they make you automatically feel you wanted to book an appointment there and then? If they did, that is a good sign. If they didn't, move on because it's likely they aren't going to light your fire. Finally, it is often useful to find out if they have published works on the topic of confidence. Take a look at their website and check to see if they have a media profile covering work around confidence and if any articles by or about them have been published, as this is often a good sign that they are an authority on the subject.

Check 3: What are their fees?

I would advise you to go for the most expensive, but this will, of course, depend on your budget. Cheap often doesn't mean bargain, but can simply mean the confidence coach is desperate for work, which is not a recipe for success. Successful people working in this business will have fees that represent their talents, so you should be prepared to pay anything from a minimum of £90 per session. Top confidence experts will often have a waiting list, so if they claim they are able to see you the following day, probe a little further by asking why they are able to offer such an immediate appointment. Remember, you want the best.

Check 4: How do they get results?

Always ask what process will be followed to achieve results. Good confidence coaches will usually utilise three models to achieve results. This may include a motivational style combined with hypnotherapy and neuro-linguistic programming (NLP). If you are unsure as to what the models mean, don't be afraid to ask and if you aren't satisfied or you are blinded with science, move on. If the confidence coach uses just one model to get results, again move on and make further enquiries.

Check 5: How many sessions are needed?

A top confidence coach will normally suggest that initially you need to attend three sessions. Results can be attained within a three-week period, as it takes around 21 days for new confidence habits to take place. If they claim you need to book more than three sessions, simply refuse. Also, do note that a leading confidence coach may ask for a non-refundable deposit to confirm your first session.

Check 6: How dedicated are they to their work?

A good coach will work in practice full time. It has to be their passion and not something they do in between doing the washing or just at weekends because they have a full-time job. In addition, they will normally have the flexibility to see you out of normal office hours to accommodate your needs. When you make your initial call, ask what hours they work and check they can fit around your schedule.

The relationship

The relationship you have with your confidence coach should be based on a set of guiding principles:

- Rapport: both parties should be comfortable, compatible and in sync with each other.

- Honesty: both parties should be constructively open with one another.

- Respect: both parties should respect each other.

- Challenge: the confidence coach should challenge where needed, in the interests of attaining a result for the client, and the client should always maintain the right to challenge the coach if needed.

- Committed: both parties should be dedicated to the coaching process to help achieve the goal.

Your responsibility

It is no good paying to work with a confidence coach thinking that they will wave a magic wand and all will come good. It simply doesn't happen like that. It is your responsibility to be motivated and positive, and this can include having an open mind and completing any homework tasks given. I always make a point of explaining to my own clients that if they bring 50 per cent of the motivation needed to the session, I will give them the remaining 50 per cent.

> " It is your responsibility to be motivated and positive "

Become a Confidence Captain

21

Now that you have worked hard, taken responsibility and improved your confidence and self-esteem, how about lending a helping hand to those who struggle with a lack of confidence and would be only too pleased to receive your help? In other words, become a confidence captain to friends, partners, relatives and colleagues. Not only will you gain great satisfaction seeing someone flourish, you will also gain a sense of personal confidence for yourself, knowing that you have inspired another human being. To aid this process, I have set out a five-step process that you can follow when supporting someone else's confidence.

Step 1: Be certain you can help

Before you set out to help someone increase their confidence, be certain that what they are asking you to do is possible. Never get involved in helping someone who is suffering from clinical depression or epilepsy, as the hypnotic techniques described in this book are never to be used with these medical conditions. Once you have established that you can help, it is useful to set goal and time ground rules for the helping relationship. But do remember that you must always refer someone who has a deeper confidence issue requiring support from a trained professional.

> **Become a confidence captain to friends, partners, relatives and colleagues**

Step 2: Encourage personal responsibility

Lending a helping hand to someone is great, but do remember that at the end of the day it is their personal responsibility. You can't *make* someone confident; all you can do is give them a helping hand, so make sure you spell this out. If you sense that there is an expectation for you to wave a magic wand, back off and explain that you aren't sure you can help.

Step 3: Explain the 7 secrets

You now have the knowledge of the 7 Secrets of Confidence and it is time to share them. In doing so, explain some of the recommended activities, but avoid imposing your views on which activity works best. We are all different, so it's important to allow people to find out what works for them. Explain the secrets in order and explain only one per day, so the person you are supporting can digest them fully. Explain how each secret supported your confidence, giving lots of practical examples, and set deadlines with the person for carrying out specific actions aligned to each of the 7 Secrets.

Step 4: Monitor and evaluate

It's all well and good to explain the 7 Secrets and agree actions against each of them, but if nothing is done then your efforts will have been pointless. It is therefore important to monitor progress and offer constructive feedback, to help ensure the person is staying on the right track to build their confidence.

Giving and receiving feedback can be problematic if you are not skilled at it, as people often struggle to do either effectively. It is important to remember that feedback is a two-way process, so it's not all about you doing the talking. Knowing how to receive feedback will also help you to be a more effective confidence captain.

Before giving any kind of feedback, it is important to establish what the person thinks about their progress in line with the 7 Secrets, so get them to carry out a self-assessment first. This will provide a great starting point for dialogue, and will also send out the message that this isn't all about you acting as the headmaster! Make sure you prepare in advance and know specifically what you want to say, as well as what you want to encourage the person to change or achieve. Make sure your feedback is plain-speaking, specific, descriptive and non-judgemental and always give examples to back up what you say. Do make sure the feedback is balanced, being sure to praise good progress as well as pointing out areas that require further work.

Step 5: Congratulate and celebrate

With good progress made, it is important to encourage the person to celebrate success. You should congratulate them and plan together something special that will celebrate and affirm the progress that has been made. This may sound a bit cheesy, but it's important. After all, if the person has got off their arse, worked hard and achieved, surely they deserve to be rewarded in some way.

Confidence captain: the key skills

If you do intend to support others, it's important you develop a number of critical skills. The steps above describe a process you can follow, but executing it means you will need to have perfected a number of key skills, including being:

Patient: being able to take your time and allow people to go at a pace that suits them best.

Supportive: offering a helping hand even when you are feeling totally frustrated or even irritated.

Interested: having a genuine interest that is real rather than fake.

A good listener: mastering the art of listening for 80 per cent of the time and talking for the remaining 20 per cent.

Perceptive: being able to tune in to what you observe.

Challenging: constructively challenging when you disagree in an assertive rather than aggressive manner.

Self-aware: ensuring you are totally aware of your impact on other people and adjusting this as necessary to enhance the relationship.

Attentive: being focused on the other person.

Retentive: remembering key information to aid the process.

A word of caution

Before deciding to confidence captain someone, do make sure you think through whether or not it is appropriate. The last thing you want to do is to start something you can't finish or realise halfway through that what set out to be a hand of support has ended in a frosty relationship. Dynamics can change when the relationship between two people becomes a little deeper. With that in mind, it can be useful to set out some ground rules to guide the confidence captain process. For example, it can be useful to agree from the outset that if either of you want to stop working on the process, you can do that. Also, agree to offer each other mutual respect as the process progresses.

Confidence captain to your kids

Being childless, I can only look at the theory behind the importance of nurturing confidence in children, but I know it is absolutely vital and I see how it impacts on the kids my relatives have.

Child psychologist Paul Mawer explains a number of practical tips for parents to ensure a child's confidence blossoms. He believes it is critical to discuss your child's day with them and have meal times together, as this encourages discussions. He also thinks it is important to give children little jobs and responsibilities. He is a fan of the copycat secret, advising that parents should get the child to identify who is confident in the class and ask what makes them think this, what does the child do and so on. See if your child can incorporate any of that confident child's behavioural repertoire into his or her own. My favourite tip is to get the kids to smile at five people a day, as people will often smile back, reinforcing the child's self-worth.

Sheila Warner, an educational psychologist (www.actpsycho logy.co.uk), offers a useful plan to help parents to become confidence captains to their children:

7 Secrets of Confidence

1 Help children to understand that all people are different and to develop a respect for others who are different. This helps them to understand that they have their own skills, strengths and so on which may be different from those of their siblings or friends.

2 Praise for 'being' as well as 'doing'. Most praise is given for something that has been done (e.g. praise for a good piece of work) rather than for being (e.g. praise for being kind, helpful, funny). What tends to happen is that bright children get praised for doing and children who struggle get praised for being, but those in the middle are overlooked.

3 Criticise the action, not the child. When a child does something for which they are in trouble, never criticise the child – so say, 'That was not a very nice thing to do' or 'That was a naughty thing to do,' rather than 'You are horrible' or 'You are naughty.'

4 Never use negative wording, such as 'stupid' or 'silly', to describe a child. As stated above, the action might be silly, but the child is not.

5 Encouragement works better than punishment. To discipline children, praise the actions that you do want rather than constantly shouting about what you don't want. So if you want children to sit at the table to eat their meals, praise and reward them for doing this, rather than concentrating on shouting at them when they are not sitting at the table.

6 Measure their progress, rather than comparing them to others. Help them to see what progress they have made and praise and encourage this.

7 Help them to understand what they are good at and what you like about them.

8 Accept what they have done and use it as a basis for improvement if this is needed. For example, say things like: 'That is a good idea, but can you think of a better one?' or 'That is a good try, but can you think of a better way to do it?'

9 Accept that their fears are valid. You may think it is stupid to be afraid of a tiny dog, but if the child is afraid, telling them that they are stupid is not going to stop their fears.

10 Help children to express their views and take them seriously.

11 Help children to make choices from an early age. For example, let them choose what they wear, let them sometimes choose where to go for a family outing, let them sometimes choose what to eat. Later on, you can encourage them to make more important choices, so that they will know how to make their own decisions as adults.

315

Question Time

Over the years, I have, quite rightly, been asked numerous questions by individuals and the media about the topic of confidence. Some of the questions were about what qualifies me to offer advice on confidence, and others on specific issues which impact on how confident a person is or can be.

You probably have some of your own questions by now, which I hope will be answered in this chapter. If they are not, just email your question to me at info@stevemillertraining.com

1   Can anyone be confident?
It is my total belief that anyone who is of sound mental state can become confident, even if they say they have lost all their confidence. However, people need to have the motivation, focus and commitment to put in the effort to help build their confidence, otherwise it simply will not happen. If they don't want to build their confidence, it can't be done.

2 What are the main blockages that can stop someone becoming confident?

A lazy, can't-be-bothered attitude and/or an individual who has built up more excuses for not being confident than reasons for going for it. If someone has the passion to become confident, it can happen.

3 How can someone develop confidence who has had years of put-downs?

By using the first secret described in this book. I fully appreciate that the past shapes us for the future, but lines have to be drawn. For many people, delving deep into the past may only make things a lot worse; we need to learn to move on from experiences, be they good or bad, because that's exactly all it is: 'experience'.

4 You yourself have had your own experience of being unconfident. During those times, did you ever think you'd never be confident again?

Occasionally I had thoughts that it may not happen, but I kept reminding myself that I was going to get there. I remained determined to rebuild my confidence and, with the support of clinical hypnotherapy, my life was changed for the better. I now believe this can happen for other people and I help ensure it does.

5 How would you describe your confidence-building process?

My process utilises the 7 Secrets. In terms of facilitation, I use confidence coaching, clinical hypnotherapy and motivational action-planning.

6 Is it naive to think that you can be fully confident in all situations, all the time?

We all have choices. We actually choose to become confident, or not, as the situation demands, but I think we all have moments where our confidence will let us down a little. The important thing is to recover from the situation, learn a lesson and make sure you are confident of dealing with whatever else life throws at you.

7 Does someone need to use all the 7 Secrets to build their confidence?

No. The secrets are tools and when repairing something for the better, you only use the appropriate tools that will fix that particular problem.

8 Is it possible to build confidence if you are constantly around people who put you down?

Definitely. In fact, you will probably find that those who put you down stop doing so because they respect your new confidence.

9 What is hypnosis and hypnotherapy?

Hypnosis is a relaxed state with an associated mental focus. It is a pleasant experience and will also help you learn to relax. Hypnotherapy is the process by which beneficial suggestions are constructed to help remove unwanted thoughts, behaviours and feelings and replace them with a positive dynamic state.

10 Is hypnotherapy safe?
It is very safe. However, I would never advocate using clinical hypnotherapy with clients suffering from clinical depression and epilepsy.

11 How does hypnotherapy cure panic attacks?
Hypnosis and hypnotherapy are very effective treatments to help cure panic attacks because they bring back the conscious control over the attacks themselves. Clients generally attend six sessions, over which time they begin to feel a sense of relief from the panic symptoms. Clients are taught self-hypnosis, so that they can carry out a number of homework tasks designed to cure the panic attacks.

12 How many sessions do clients attend if they are looking to build their confidence?
My standard confidence-building programme includes attendance at three sessions.

13 What kinds of people do you work with?
Over the years, I have worked with people from all walks of life, including office managers, company directors, actors, teachers, mums, television presenters, bank staff, entrepreneurs, sports professionals, builders and soldiers.

14 If there was one piece of advice you were to give someone struggling with their confidence what would it be?

I would say take a deep breath and relax and just start to think calmly and rationally about being confident in the next moments, minutes, hours, days, years. A confident state of mind is one in which we accept that we are all imperfect and that we all have opportunities to shine.

15 What is your most memorable story when helping someone to build their confidence?

This has to be a guy who I supported over just three sessions. He was a professional chap and at the first session he looked miserable, dour and talked of himself as a complete failure. After the three sessions, he lost weight, improved his image, strengthened his self-belief, began dating a woman he'd had his eye on for many months, proposed to her and confidently invited me to the wedding!

16 Do you run confidence courses for companies?

Yes, and I ensure I incorporate how to develop confidence in all of my management and sales training programmes. We have to remember that people will only use the skills if they have the confidence. I also enjoy corporate and motivational speaking. It's great to see the lightbulb being switched on when people grasp a concept or technique that will help them move forward in their life.

17 Do you ever get nervous?

Of course I do. We are all fallible. When I get nervous, I

channel it in the right way. I make sure I reframe the nerves and turn them into feelings of excitement and confidence.

18 Do you think most people can achieve their dreams?
Absolutely! But it takes hard work and personal motivation. Sadly, most people talk about dreams but do nothing to make them turn into reality. You have probably gathered by now that I am an action-driven guy. Talk without action achieves NOWT.

19 What do you do to ensure you maintain your confidence?
Every day I will do something to maintain confidence. I live my life by the 7 Secrets and apply them as needed.

20 If I had just one day to build my confidence, what would you advise?
There are three things you must do. Firstly, perceive yourself as high street, not back street. Secondly, affirm the belief in yourself and visualise yourself being totally confident. Finally, ensure you are branded brilliantly and act as if you are confident.

21 What are you like to work with as a confidence coach?
Straight-talking, action-focused, motivational, light-hearted and, of course, on your side.

22 How can I find out more?
Visit www.stevemillertraining.com

A Few Final Words

You have probably by now begun to adopt the 7 Secrets of Confidence, and it's important to continue to enjoy the journey as your confidence reaches new heights.

The benefits you reap from your expanding confidence will continue to build all the time and life is going to be very different – for the better, of course. So much comes from being confident, and it's important you don't feel guilty, especially if those around you are clearly not confident little bunnies like you. They may envy you (remember, not a bad thing) or be jealous. If it's the latter and they are trying to drag you back down to their level, just ignore them. Instead, enjoy the journey and occasionally spoil yourself for the work you did in following the 7 Secrets. Remind yourself that *you* did it and no one else. You will probably have found that some things are a little tough and others pretty straightforward, but at the end of the day you made the effort.

The reactions from others will be a revelation to you and them. There will be those who support your new-found confidence and others who, through their own stinking jealousy, want to pull you down and trip you up. Experience tells me that as you grow in confidence, you will be met with claims of how much you have changed for the better or the worse. Those who stroke your new confidence are friends and family to keep around you, whereas those who try to poison your growth should be ditched and, yes, at times that may include partners. Becoming confident and achieving new heights does mean some tough decisions may have to be made with regard to personal relationships.

As confidence grows and your self-esteem reaches heights that you could only once dream of, it's important to keep yourself in check. Arrogance is a quality I boo; confidence is one I applaud. Remember that confident people are assertive, they have an opinion and they have a great self-belief, but at the same time they appreciate and support those around them. Arrogant people are opinionated and they absolutely hate to listen to the views of others. You will notice that they continually fail to take any interest in or support the lives of other people. In other words, they have an attitude that says, 'I'm okay; you're not okay,' whereas confident and assertive people have the philosophy of 'I'm okay; you're okay too.'

So it's perfectly okay to celebrate the new you, reward yourself hugely and expect good things to happen, but never, never, never open the door to arrogance, otherwise the cracks will very soon start to appear and you may well start to suffer the consequences of malicious words and actions from the jealous brigade.

For a personal consultation with me, email me at info@stevemillertraining.com Further information may be found at www.stevemillertraining.com.

Further Reading

Confidence: The Art of Getting Whatever You Want, Dr Rob Yeung (Prentice Hall Life 2008)

Feel the Fear and Do It Anyway, Susan Jeffers (Vermilion 2007)

How to Win Friends and Influence People, Dale Carnegie (Vermilion 2007)

How to Talk to Anyone, Leil Lowndes (Thorsons 2008)

Building Self-confidence for Dummies, Kate Burton and Brinley Platts (John Wiley & Sons 2005)

The Confidence Plan, Sarah Litvinoff (BBC Active 2007)

Persuasion: The Art of Influencing People, James Borg (Prentice Hall 2007)

Other helpful sources of information and advice

http://www.bsch.org.uk/ – The British Society of Clinical Hypnosis

http://www.hypnotherapysociety.com/ – The Hypnotherapy Society

http://www.associationforcoaching.com/pub/pub03.htm – Help with finding a life coach

http://www.coachfederation.org.uk/ – The International Coach Federation

http://www.nhs.uk/LiveWell/loseweight – Advice on losing weight

http://www.mentalhealth.org.uk/campaigns/look-after-your-mental-health/ – Advice on mental health issues

http://www.bbc.co.uk/relationships/improving_your_confidence/links_index.shtml – Other useful sources